Street Children
in Kenya

Street Children in Kenya

Voices of Children in Search of a Childhood

Philip Kilbride, Collette Suda, and Enos Njeru

BERGIN & GARVEY
Westport, Connecticut • London

Library of Congress Cataloging-in-Publication Data

Kilbride, Philip Leroy.
    Street children in Kenya : voices of children in search of a childhood / Philip Kilbride,
Collette Suda, and Enos Njeru.
        p.   cm.
    Includes bibliographical references and index.
    ISBN 0–89789–529–0 (alk. paper)—ISBN 0–89789–862–1 (pbk.)
    1. Street children—Kenya.   I. Suda, Collette A.   II. Njeru, Enos Hudson Nthia.   III. Title.
    HV887.K4 K55   2000
    305.9′06′945096762—dc21   99–046150

British Library Cataloguing in Publication Data is available.

Library of Congress Catalog Card Number: 99–046150
ISBN: 0–89789–862–1 (pbk.)

First published in 2000

Bergin & Garvey, 88 Post Road West, Westport, CT 06881
An imprint of Greenwood Publishing Group, Inc.
www.greenwood.com

Printed in the United States of America

The paper used in this book complies with the
Permanent Paper Standard issued by the National
Information Standards Organization (Z39.48–1984).

10 9 8 7 6 5 4 3 2 1

We dedicate this book to the children of the street children of Nairobi; may their social conditions be better than those of their parents.

Contents

Tables

Preface

This book results from a cross-national and interdisciplinary research effort. Although Collette Suda (C. S.), a rural sociologist, and Enos Njeru (E. N.), and Philip Kilbride (P. K.), both anthropologists, were all academically trained in the United States, we have benefited from an "insider"–"outsider" dialogue in writing this book. C. S. and E. N., as Kenyans, kept our work closely grounded in local language, cultural interpretations, and applied recommendations. P. K. focused on ethnography as an "outsider," as non-Kenyans must do, and also sought to coordinate our findings with comparative, cultural, and theoretical concerns beyond the Kenyan scene. We operated, however, on some occasions as insiders or outsiders given P. K.'s research on children and family in East Africa since 1967 and E. N.'s and C. S.'s international travel, education, and living experiences abroad. More details about our collaboration in research and writing together are provided in the text.

Street children are often portrayed by the public and sometimes in publications as a separate, socially distinct category of person. We have tried to emphasize here social complexities that problemtize this simplistic view. Following a holistic perspective, we have emphasized throughout the book how street children in Kenya, in fact, live like other Kenyans, embedded, for example, in similar institutions, informal work routines, cultural beliefs, and family relations. Such involvements are not dissimilar in many respects from others who make up the working poor in Nairobi. Still, street children do stand apart as a distinct social category both in their own minds and that of the public as well. We will consider reasons for this and which social characteristics seem widely shared among street children. Throughout, however, while recognizing commonalities, we attempt to emphasize the rich variation among children that we discovered in our research.

In our book we seek to systematically provide information about street girls. An awareness of difference and variation as our work progressed compelled us to emphasize gender differences at every turn. We also wanted to highlight gender inasmuch as compared to boys, very little is published about street girls. This is strikingly true in Kenya but, to a great degree, elsewhere in the world as well. We decided to incorporate a gendered analysis throughout the book rather than providing separate chapters on girls. This decision was taken so as to better put across the idea that there are commonalities among all street children irrespective of gender differences. When all is said and done, boys and girls in Kenya share a common label and many similar problems.

As part of our holistic perspective, we have taken special note of how the current problem of street children in Kenya stands in sharp contrast to indigenous derived practices and experiences associated with childhood in Kenya. The street child is but a recent event in the culture history of Kenya. Specifically, we have emphasized Kenyan family cultural beliefs and indigenous practices as an interpretive framework not only because we believe this to be relevant, but also inasmuch as family and gender issues themselves, apart from street children, have occupied us prior to and throughout our work with street children. For better or worse, we have tried here to relate social topics we know the most about to the situation of street children. Only the reader can judge if we have overstated our family-friendly interpretation and related practical recommendations with which we conclude this book. We trust that most readers will agree that family analysis is certainly relevant to a full understanding of street children in Kenya. Whatever interpretive conclusions arise on this point, we all hope that our descriptive materials about street children stand alone and are informative in their own right.

Throughout our research and writing, we have followed research methods that attempt to involve the voices of street children concerning events, beliefs, experiences, and aspirations that they privilege in their own discourse about themselves. Ethnography, focus group, and social survey converge around our experience near research methodology. Overall, previous published materials in Kenya have not systematically privileged children's voices in the multimethod sense that we have attempted here. Nevertheless, we have also set out theoretical objectives and conceptual categories derived from our own disciplinary, theoretical concerns and comparative understandings about street children globally. Therefore, we will consider interplay between children's voices and our theoretical framework as part of our discussion of methodology.

However, inclusion of street children's voices here is more than simply a matter of epistemology. Our ultimate intention of being able to better suggest some applied, practical recommendations to policy makers also compels us to consider children's perspectives wherever possible. It is unlikely that many policy recommendations concerning street children will get very far before people first learn directly from the children about themselves. How best to assist them is also something street children have thought about and about which they have strong opinions. We end our book with policy recommendations that take into account, but which are not limited to, the voices of those children represented in our research. We are hopeful that our recommendations, about social policy and applications of our research in Kenya will be of interest to all of those thinking about applied solutions to what is, in fact, a global problem concerning street children in many nations.

We use pseudonyms in this book for most individuals whom we encountered in fieldwork. In particular, we have used real or invented nicknames for all street children on the advice of street children who, themselves, use nicknames to conceal their identities from the police. An exception is "Mama Ford," a buyer of waste products from street boys who, after reading what we had written about her with approval, requested that we give her real name, Josephine Karanja, in publication.

We have also not published photographs so as to conceal the identities of street children, most of whom are regularly under harassment from the police. Moreover, most street children may want their past lives on the streets kept private in the future. There is a rapid turnover on the streets such that as far as the street children described here are concerned, all have left the streets or now live in different locations in Nairobi. The wheel of field research and publication grinds slowly; in our case, that has served our desire to protect the identities of our informants as well as to become familiar with changes in their lives over time.

Acknowledgments

This book results from a cross-national collaboration. Philip Kilbride and Enos Njeru began research together in 1993 and continued their work on street children in 1994 with support from the National Science Foundation. We are grateful to the NSF and also to Priscilla Kariuki and Lewis Aptekar, our co-investigators on that project, which set in motion subsequent work until the summer of 1999, when our field research ended. Over the years, Bryn Mawr and Haverford College students conducted college ethnographic fieldwork under the supervision of Philip Kilbride on various topics concerning street children. We profited from our discussion with these former Bryn Mawr College anthropology students and would like to thank Elizabeth Tunstall, Caryn Groce, Marie Horchler, Ami Rae Adams, Vera Limcuando, Fatima Humera, and Alison Mott. We appreciate research funds from Bryn Mawr College, which made possible student research and also the ethnographic fieldwork of Philip Kilbride over five summers and one sabbatical semester. The Institute of African Studies, University of Nairobi is acknowledged here for their sponsorship of our field projects. The president's office in Kenya is thanked for permission to conduct field research among street children.

Collette Suda joined Philip Kilbride and Enos Njeru in 1996 to write this book. We combined our field data in ways set out in the book and developed together a general framework and specific ideas from our data to prioritize here. Philip Kilbride wrote our first working draft, with subsequent editorial revisions by his co-authors. Collette Suda conducted a social survey of street children in 1994. Partial results from this survey and related research are incorporated into this book, specifically contextualized by Philip Kilbride with data and unpublished papers contributed by Philip Kilbride and Enos Njeru and themes developed by the three of us together. Collette Suda would like to acknowledge the assistance and support of those involved with her survey. She thanks the Child Welfare Society of Kenya, specifically Mr. Munene Kahiro, Mr. Kahura,

Mrs. N. W. Nyala, and Mrs. Elizabeth Oyugi. The research assistance and tireless efforts of Ms. Veronicah Oduol and Mr. Difas Shitakwu are appreciated. The children, parents, and leaders of nongovernmental organizations, who provided information, are gratefully acknowledged here for their time, patience, and cooperation during the survey.

Philip Kilbride and Enos Njeru thank those who cooperated with us in focus group sessions concerning their views about street children. Samuel William Kikiku wrote a thoughtful essay as a follow up to his focus group participation. Mr. Michael Andolo served Philip Kilbride as an able and insightful research assistant. Mr. Ambroise Otieno was helpful and a source of inspiration. We thank Drs. Janet Kilbride, Steve Ferzacca, and Mary Doi for their valuable suggestions on an earlier draft of this book. Drs. John Andrew Brook and Jim Baumohl are thanked for their references.

Philip Kilbride gratefully acknowledges Dr. Douglas Davis, who ably helped with student projects. Dr. Robert Washington shared his observations about street children in Kenya. Faculty and students at Bryn Mawr College, Washington College, Lincoln University, and the University of Nevada–Las Vegas made many insightful comments in response to invited lectures by Philip Kilbride concerning street girls in Nairobi. Of these, Drs. William Jankowiak, Penny Swartz, and Emmanuel Babatunde are especially thanked. Jane Garry, Editor for Anthropology, Greenwood Publishing Group, is warmly thanked for her support of our book project. Dr. Janet Kilbride provided editorial assistance commensurate with her sharp eye for detail, especially concerning African children. We are indebted to Karen Sulpizio for her superb secretarial work on various drafts. We appreciate all the suggestions and assistance acknowledged here and, of course, accept sole responsibility for our interpretations.

We are especially grateful to the many street children who worked with us, some as research assistants and others as informants and respondents or who otherwise opened up their lives to us through observation and informal discussions. We have tried to respond to their kindness by doing our best to complete this book to the best of our ability. Some of the children had hoped we would make public their views, and we have tried to do so, notwithstanding shortcomings, the usual ones in social research and also those inherent in the obvious difficulties in work of the sort described here.

Chapter 1

Introduction: Kenyan Street Children from a Local and Global Perspective

A child of ten years of age ran behind a small toy object made of wire, wood and maize cobs. The "car" also had a wire passenger with head and arms in "conversation" with the boy, whose dialogue could be inferred from his moving lips and focused attention on his "car." The street was crowded with late afternoon pedestrians who seemingly hardly noticed the street boy as he moved among them with an apparent clear sense of where he was heading. Following along behind him for a short time, I soon found myself at the boy's "roundabout" destination. It was a grassy elevation surrounded by a circular highway around which rapidly moving vehicles of various sizes, shapes, and colors competed for entrance onto one of four highways for an opportunity to continue on their way to destinations distant and local. Just before his arrival at the peri-urban roundabout, other boys who were stretched out resting on the elevated terrain on which they ate and slept greeted the child. Just before crossing the road, circling the roundabout, the boy scooped his toy into his small hands as he dodged a car to reach the safety of his "home," the place where he sleeps and sometimes cooks scavenged potatoes and other vegetables with his cohorts. In the background could be heard noises from closely passing vehicles that emanated foul-smelling fumes, to which the children had become accustomed. His companions, about ten in number, dressed in torn clothing and barefooted, warmly greeted him. As he set down his toy he picked up a small bottle and joined the others in sniffing glue. (Kilbride field notes, 1995)

There are recurring features in the lives of street children everywhere in the world, including Kenya. First, and most importantly, it should be emphasized that street children are, in fact, children! Child behaviors like playing with toys, crying, and sucking of thumbs, for example, are likely to go unnoticed amongst routine "adult" activities which are common among street children globally (Glasser, 1994). Childlike status is not readily apparent among such worldwide pursuits as survival sex (prostitution) among street girls and working as garbage collectors among street boys, not to mention a seemingly adultlike "freedom," with independence from adult authority typical of most street children around the world (Aptekar, 1988). Street children range in age from newborn infants born on the streets up to about 16 to 18 years of age when most nations define the person as an adult. Nevertheless, as we shall see, Kenyan "street children" sometimes include boys in their mid-20s, although this is rare. The majority of the world's street children are boys, including Kenya's.

The boy with the toy at the beginning of this chapter, like many of the approximately 100 million street children in the world, is a boy "of" the streets (Campos et al., 1994). These children "of" the streets regularly sleep outdoors away from home. Homeless street children who can be found sleeping outdoors in such places as alleys, street pavements, store fronts and roundabouts comprise about 20% of the world's street children (Glasser, 1994). As elsewhere, the majority of street children in Kenya (about 80%), return home to sleep frequently enough to be thought of as children "on" the streets where they daily eke out a living.

The boy with the toy and his companions were eating scavenged food, such things as throwaway vegetables from open-air food stalls and eggs, bread, and meat discarded from restaurants. Food scavenging is a behavior Nairobi street children share with street children around the world. Be it digging in garbage dumps or picking scraps from market places, street children commonly face a constant struggle to get food, a task that is often problematic in an urban environment. Street children do not participate in customary patterns of familial food exchange typical of most Kenyans (Kilbride & Kilbride, 1990). In Kenya, street children are known as *chokora*, roughly translated from Kiswahili as pokers at dustbins or garbage heaps in search of food and other valuables. An earlier generation of street boys were known as "parking boys," named for their assistance in guarding and parking cars. *Chokora* as a verb in Kiswahili means "to pick "or "to poke." Accordingly, Kenyans describe street boys as ones who "grab inside" or "pull down," as if from a dustbin or garbage can. One boy, for example, noted that "What makes us to be called *chokora* is that we always pick litter and go to rubbish pits in the process." *Chokora* as a noun refers to a "kitchen boy," one who does odd jobs. In either usage, an association with food is suggested.

Kenyan street children were frequently observed sniffing glue, as do street children worldwide who often develop addictions to glue and other substances. The "glue bottle" in the public mind negatively symbolizes what is taken to be, in Kenya and often elsewhere, the defining characteristic of street children: that is, people who are troublemakers and a threat to society. Hidden behind the bottle, in fact, can be observed a child's face, a child who frequently, as we shall see, works like an adult for survival. Significantly, in her overview of street children worldwide, Irene Glasser (1994) concludes, "The words used for street children often reflect the jobs they do" (p. 61). She describes, for example, the Khate in Katmandu, Nepal, who live by collecting trash for sale and the "parking boys" of Kenya. We will follow Glasser's term "survival sex" (p. 76), a term for child prostitution, illicit work practiced widely by street girls in order to emphasize the lack of choice that such prostitution entails for them as their only viable means of living on the streets.

A striking finding in our research, as indicated from the example above, is the many similarities between street children in our study and their counterparts elsewhere. We endorse Johann Le Roux's (1996) conclusion, based on research in South Africa, that "it needs to be emphasized that street children represent a worldwide phenomenon despite cultural differences. Examination of the literature also indicates that the backgrounds of street children . . . are remarkably similar . . . findings presented in the present study . . . are common among street children internationally" (p. 430). Widespread similarities among street children prompt one to ask "Why so?" Without doubt, the phenomenal growth of the international economy with demands of the global economy for competitive prices has served to pressure local markets for cheap labor, often including children as laborers. Nancy Scheper-Hughes and Carolyn Sargent (1998, p. 12) have observed that children, who once "worked" in the context of home communities, now "labor" in industrial and global capitalism. At the same time, they and others point to structural adjustment policies meant to stabilize state economies, which have seriously burdened the poorest populations, especially women and children. Tobias Hecht (1998) believes that some recurring elements in the global paradigm of childhood include the only feasible and approved habitats for children of school, home, and commercial play places, such as shopping malls and amusement parks. He thinks that this approved habitat specialization follows from a market-based world combined with state-regulated education to prepare children for the workforce. Hecht (1998) points out that street children are, as it were, occupants of a prohibited space. Concerning his own work, he concludes, "Brazil's street children challenge the hierarchical worlds of home and school and threaten the commercialized "public" space such as stores and shopping centers. . . . They subvert their country's . . . social apartheid that keeps the poor . . . out of view" (p. 211). Hecht's perceptive insights are echoed in David Wagner's (1993) observation that "Homelessness can be seen as both causing and being reflective of a broader legitimization crisis in modern society" (p. 10). The stigmatized social status of Kenya's street children, like that of their counterparts elsewhere, can be seen in constant police harassment and public fear of them, symbolic of their lives lived apart from school, family, and community in contrast to legitimate social contexts for children.

The geographic movement of industries from the modern welfare states, while contributing to deindustrialization, poverty, and homelessness in them, brought a similarly exploitative factory-based, economic presence in countries where employers moved in search of cheap labor (Susser, 1996). While Kenyan street children do not work in factories, some have run away from industrial plantations where they have worked as exploited children. Additionally, they have been impacted directly by industrial waste that pollutes their home space on the streets. Moreover, addiction to glue has followed directly from the development of shoe industries in various countries. Scheper-Hughes and Hoffman (1998) report that the addiction of Brazilian street children to glue sniffing resulted from glue obtained from local shoe factories. We will discuss reasons that Nairobi street boys and girls inhale glue, but in the present context it is significant that the reasons they gave us were similar to what street children reported in Brazil, including making life better by dulling hunger, by helping to forget problems, and by giving courage to face dangers (Campos et al., 1994, p. 325). While there are powerful constraints in the life circumstances and the adjustments of street children worldwide, there are also impressive differences that not only reflect cultural distinctions but also profound variation among individuals in terms of personality, temperament, and life choices. We will illustrate such differences where personal profiles of individual children will be presented. Presently, street children on the continent of Africa will provide a good basis for discussion of variation which, along with similarities, needs also to be emphasized.

Street children in Africa are a recent development but frequently reflect patterns of exploitation emanating from colonialism in the early 20th century. In Dar es Salaam, Tanzania, for example, there were between 200 and 300 street children in 1991, but by 1995 there were 3,500 (Bamurange, 1998, p. 230). In 1984, in Khartoum, Sudan, street children were limited to a few boys only, but by 1990, "street boys were a predictable part of the urban landscape" (Dodge & Raundalen, 1991, p. 40). In South Africa, all street children are of African origin, with no white children on the streets, a fact reflective of South Africa's history of racial segregation and apartheid (Le Roux, 1996). Kenya too has no Asian or European street children, a reflection of racism during colonialism up to the early 1960s. While in 1969 Kenya had only a few hundred "parking boys," today, there are an estimated 10,000 to 30,000 street children in Nairobi. Throughout Africa, street boys greatly outnumber street girls. Girls, for example, are expected to stay home to care for children in South Africa (Le Roux, 1996, p. 426). In Khartoum and Maputo, Mozambique, girls were placed in homes as servants and punished if they moved to the streets (Dodge & Raundalen, 1991, p. 43). Later, we will discuss gender distinctions among Nairobi's street children.

There are specific macro causes that are associated with a dramatic rise in Africa's street children, along with the poverty of global economic and structural adjustment forces mentioned above. These factors include civil war and famine such as in Mozambique and Sudan, (Dodge & Raundalen, 1991), children soldiers and AIDS in Uganda, (Dodge & Raundalen, 1991; Kilbride &

Kilbride, 1990), and apartheid in South Africa (Le Roux, 1996). All of these common African patterns are at work in Kenya, too.

Whatever the macro causes, virtually all writers concerned with African street children report family breakdown as the immediate precipitating push factor that prompts a child to leave home directly for the streets or eventually to arrive there as a child "of" the streets (Dodge & Raundalen, 1991; Bamurange, 1998; Le Roux, 1996). In our research, too, family troubles at home, especially the absence of a father, proved to be a powerful push factor to the streets. For this reason, we will discuss why we believe a cultural model, one emphasizing the extended family, is appropriate for better understanding of the social situation of street children in Kenya and perhaps elsewhere in Africa.

It would appear that African family life, one in which a strong male authority figure is emphasized, usually the father, provides a sharp contrast to some other parts of the world. (See especially Virginia Bamurange, 1998, pp. 230–34, where father absences are notable.) Lewis Aptekar (1988) argues that a common "matrifocal" (mother-headed) family structure in Colombia socializes boys to leave home around puberty and make their living on the streets. Some street boys are, therefore, best seen as "normal" within the context of a family structure at odds with the more patriarchal family form idealized in the dominant Hispanic-derived familial culture of Colombia. In our research, a matrifocal tendency has resulted in an aberrant movement of children away from homes that no longer adequately provide for them. The same social structure can have drastically different consequences for children living under different cultural systems.

Variation can be seen too among African cases in overall adjustment of street children to life on the streets depending on various cultural circumstances that have contributed to their departure for the city. Comparison between Mozambique and Sudan provides a good example. In Sudan about 10,000 children lived on Khartoum's streets in 1990 (Dodge & Raundalen, 1991). At about ten years of age, the majority of those boys were sent from the south where a civil war was raging. Although a dominant theme was a family breakup, there was an approved pattern of male migration to the city, which served as a role model for the children. Returning boys also often described the city in positive terms. Some parents encouraged their boys to leave home as one indicated, "My mother put me on a truck heading for Khartoum and said, 'I want to think that one of my children survived this war' (Dodge & Raundalen, 1991, p. 45). Like matrifocal family structure in Columbia, civil war and approved male migration can serve as push factors onto the streets, often with a resourceful adaptation there by the children after their arrival in the city. In comparison to the many resourceful adaptations described by street children in Colombia by Aptekar (1988) and by Dodge & Raundalen (1991) in Sudan, the latter in their Mozambique study report, "Almost all the street boys interviewed characterized street life as miserable" (p. 46). When asked why they left home, most told a sad tale usually involving a family tragedy or some catastrophic event related to poverty. Cultural supports for street children of the sort described here for many of the street boys in Sudan and Colombia were absent in Mozambique.

Hecht (1998) discusses variation in published views about the overall quality of life of the street children ranging from what he considers Aptekar's and others "sanguine" view to that of those who share his view derived from his work with street children in Brazil, which is epitomized in his statement about the "devastation of human life I saw in following street children closely" (p. 202). It should be noted, however, that while overall generalizations about quality of life in specific populations of street children seem justified, all studies, including our own material, find considerable variation among the children individually commensurate with their particular and *in toto* unique combinations of social and personal circumstances. Thus, there can be no typical street child or typical street children population. The individual person must always be at the forefront.

It is clear from the material considered here that "the street child" worldwide is not to be essentialized as a master status apart from specific contexts socially constructed in various historical, economic, and cultural circumstances. This is true for Kenyan street children too. We will consider street children in Kenya as best understood not so much as "street children" but as members of the working poor in this nation with whom they have much in common. Most Kenyan street children, like many other children in this country, labor in exploitative situations. Along with child housemaids, primarily girls, and child workers on plantations and in shops, street girls in Kenya work in survival prostitution and boys as car tenders, carriers of loads and groceries, and collectors of garbage for recycling. Both street boys and girls labor very hard at begging and, for this reason, we will provide information on this important but stressful coping strategy for "survival," to use the term used by street children themselves.

Just as it is useful to consider street children as members of the working poor, it is also insightful to conceive of them as a component of the growing numbers of the world's homeless population (Susser, 1966). In Kenya, the street child is frequently uprooted from family and home and sleeps outside on the streets on garbage piles and verandas, in doorways, and at roundabouts. Similar to homeless youth in Wales sleeping outside or sleeping "rough" and to adults, including mothers with children, sleeping in automobiles in the United States, many street children worldwide, including Kenya, are de-domiciled (Glasser, 1994; Snow & Anderson, 1993; Wagner, 1993; and Dehavenon, 1996). I. Susser's (1996) remark that "homeless people appear homeless rather than displaced" (p. 416) is certainly true for Kenya, where, as we shall see, street children and their families are by and large products of massive urban migration into Nairobi that has occurred since independence in Kenya in 1963. Many urban Kenyan adults and children are, in a sense, "homeless," as "home" for most Kenyans is a rural location where one intends to be buried, not the city where one has a "house" and employment. Many street children are, of course, an extreme case of such a departure from a home base since they often not only live apart from a home family but are de-domiciled as well.

We will consider the cultural construction of "home" for the Kenyan context, but at the outset it is necessary to bear in mind that ideas about home are always culturally informed. In a review of recent work on the homeless, Robert Desjarlais (1996) reminds us that "the common drawbacks of being homeless might be less in their perceived physical or phenomenal features, such as moving about, sleeping in the open, or lacking privacy from others—than in being isolated, disaffiliated, and marginalized from the social, economic, and political worlds of others" (p. 424). We will see that Kenyan street children are preoccupied as much if not more with fears of police harassment and negative reactions to them from the public as they are from any sense of being "homeless" or without food. Still, in some cases that we specify, children in our research strike us as being similar to homeless adults described elsewhere in their adaptive strategies for survival. For instance, Kenyan street children have, like American homeless adults, a strong sense of community in their social organization similar to findings of community by David Wagner (1993), and also they engage in "identity talk" as a form of social negotiation to enhance their self-esteem as noted by David Snow and Leon Anderson (1993).

Nevertheless, street children are, when all is said and done, psychologically and developmentally children. We found, however, that many of the street children in our study were extremely resourceful in their adaptive strategies such that their lives and attitudes were seemingly mature beyond their chronological years. We were struck by the sense in which many street children were psychologically "invulnerable" similar to children noted elsewhere living in stressful environments (see Anthony & Cohler, 1987 for an overview of studies of resilient children in vulnerable circumstances).   Despite the undeniable detriments of such things as oppressive parents, severe physical handicaps, and extreme poverty, and so on many children "Instead of falling victims to despair, degradation, and deficit . . . not only remain unscarred, but can function at remarkably high levels" (Anthony, p. 40).

Other researchers, like us, have concluded that street children include significantly among their numbers cases of seeming invulnerability. Virginia Bamurange (1998), for example, working in Tanzania concludes that, "All the street youths I met had similar stories to tell . . . other adolescents in normal situations do not usually form permanent links and are usually cautious about the strong emotions that accompany the maintenance of relationships" (p. 234). Cole Dodge and Magne Raundalen (1991) reached a similar conclusion for street children among whom they worked in Sudan and Mozambique: "We felt quite confident that most of them were resilient, resourceful with courage" (p. 47). Nevertheless, Dodge and Raundalen caution against viewing street children as "super" children, noting that they cannot live on dust and dirty words alone. We will consider gender differences and distinctions of life "on" the street as opposed to being "of" the street which may have a bearing on a child's relative invulnerability. Only future research can sort out this important issue.

Notwithstanding, individual capabilities and personal circumstances that distinguish street children in Kenya, for all of them the social status of "street child" is but an "event" in their lives, albeit a significant one. The public all too often essentializes the concept of street child in terms of a small number of traits thought to apply to all street children in all situations. Social labels such as "thief," "glue addict," "prostitute," "public menace," "idlers," and the like belie the behavioral complexity and personal variation behind each street child. For this reason, we want to emphasize that being a street child is "an event," one with a beginning and for most an end that culminates in a transition into some adult status. We will consider entry points onto the streets and examples of transitions after life on the streets later in this book.

Philip Salzman (1998) defines an event as a sequence of actions and consequences. He writes, "Of great interest for us is the impact an event has on people's lives, the way it redirects lives, shapes them, terminates them, liberates them. People do not live in static, stable environments" (p. 3). Such events as, for example, droughts, floods, famines, wars, depressions, and the like are all made up of constituent micro events involving people, places, and special circumstance. Profound great events such as the Irish Potato Famine, the Great Flu Epidemic of 1918, or the Holocaust are examples of big events whereas graduations, marriages, wakes, and baptisms are examples of smaller events. All events are bounded in time with a beginning and an end, and all events are subject to socially constructed cultural definitions and interpretations. Just as the Irish Potato Famine was, for example, a tragic historical event in the mid-19th century for Irish in Ireland and those in the resulting diaspora, so too is the "street child" phenomenon in Kenya a historical event, one with specific origins to be described later. One hopes that one day this ongoing event will become only a historical event, but one whose lessons will remain as with other tragic, great events mentioned here. As we shall see, childhood among Kenyan indigenous cultures offers a striking contrast to the present day profile of the street child. In short, there is nothing "essential" about African childhood or personhood that dictates that street children cannot be reduced in Kenya by utilizing cultural resources still available within indigenous traditions. We will return to this question in the last chapter, where we consider applications for social policy.

While the street child is but a current event in Kenya, and the status of street children is a temporary label endured by specific children, we will also see that street life is composed of specific recurring events, including, for example, work strategies, recreational routines, and romantic involvement amid a complex social life lived in communities with other street children. In sum, not only is the "street child" a temporary historical and personal label, but even for those who are street children, it is clear that their social lives are far more complex than the simple public label "street child" implies. We hope to convey a sense of this social complexity in the pages that follow. Specifically in our chapter on personal profiles, we follow a narrative method to set out experienced lives of some street boys and girls as they described them to us. When one considers such narratives, one is pressed to recognize the factors of variability among the children in backgrounds, aspirations, and personal dispositions. Nevertheless, in other pages where we focus on events and observed social life, there is also complexity, but at the same time more apparent similarity in overt adjustments to the demands for "surviving," as they put it, on the streets of Nairobi.

In the next chapter we will consider our research methodology, one that seeks to integrate surveys, focus group interviews, and ethnography in such a way that a significant play is given to the voices of street children themselves. Nevertheless, as we have indicated in this chapter, our approach is at the same time comparative with some analytical categories derived, where appropriate, from research elsewhere. We see no conflict in privileging local meanings while at the same time offering some generalizations where this seems reasonable. We have tried to make clear that generalizations are not to be taken as examples of an "essentializing" method. In our last chapter we will offer a "cultural model" specific to the Kenya context that represents another effort to ground our work in a culturally specific context. In our goal to offer practical suggestions for social policy within a specific historical and cultural space, we should also emphasize that the plight of Kenyan street children is simultaneously global, national, and local in scale. For this reason, many, if not most, readers of this book, as participants in our global economy, should view themselves not only as part of the problem but also as a necessary part of the solution.

Chapter 2

Methodology: Perspectives and Multiple Techniques

While I stood at a bus stage waiting for a bus to Westlands, a place where I was well known to street boys, an unfamiliar street boy of about fourteen years of age dressed in tattered clothes emerged from the crowd. Reaching to take a piece of mud, the boy stared menacingly at me, only to be faced with an equally unfriendly glare from me. After a short time, the boy broke into laughter, dropped his mud, and proceeded on his way without begging or glancing back. On another occasion, earlier on the same day at the same bus stage location, I had given ten shillings, about 20 cents, to a street boy (all I had at the time), an act of "charity" that surprisingly was greeted only with mockery as the boy disgustedly threw the coin away on the sidewalk while continuing on his way. Street boys often express to tourists such dissatisfaction with small coins. (Kilbride field notes, 1996)

ETHNOGRAPHY

These two encounters with street boys involving instances of often feigned hostility, as well as other patterned behaviors, are aptly revealed through "participant observation," a key ethnographic research technique employed in the present study (Pelto & Pelto, 1978; Bernard, 1994). The ethnographic research for this book included repeated visits involving participant observation by Philip Kilbride (P. K.) from June 1993, continuing thereafter for four more summer periods, with an additional visit in October 1995, living in the residential, periurban community of Westlands, an affluent multiracial community that is largely self-contained with numerous business and office premises. Westlands is also a home for street children who are attracted to this community as a good place for begging or collection of waste products for sale and eventual recycling (see chapter 6). P. K. lived elsewhere in Kenya in the summer of 1998 and from January to June 1999 while working on this book. Nevertheless, he made regular visits to Westlands and other locations where the street children to be described later live and work. Collette Suda (C. S.) and Enos Njeru (E. N.), as Kenyans, have encountered street children not only in our research but also in the course of "participating" for many years in their daily lives in the city of Nairobi, at markets, shopping centers, and while walking on streets. Our conversations together served as a cross-check on the participatory ethnographic material reported in this book as experienced by P. K.

None of us, however, participated directly in the social activities of street children such as sleeping outdoors and begging. Nevertheless, we did profit by our participation as adults in social roles reciprocal to those relationships forged by street children with outsiders necessary for their survival. P. K., in particular, by virtue of consistently "being there" (Geertz, 1988, pp. 1–25; Agar, 1996, p. 31) so regularly on the streets in Westlands was able as an ethnographer to better observe social life as it routinely and sometimes unexpectantly unfolded over time in a community that after a while took his presence among them day or night as routine. Moreover, while he slept away from the street children and did not participate in most of their activities, he did enjoy with them many conversations, meals, and recreational activities such as football and cards. Mobility is severely limited at night. Kenyans rarely venture into the streets after dark for fear of thieves or personal attack. Nevertheless, in time P. K. felt much less fear at night when in the company of street boys. In fact, the only direct threat he encountered was an organized pickpocket attempt by three thieves on a crowded stagecoach bus during a lunch rush hour. P. K. stopped the attempt by feigning that he would shout "thief," which would have resulted in a "mob justice" intervention by fellow passengers. His wallet was immediately returned.

Compensation as reciprocity is crucial in fieldwork undertaken by visiting social scientists in Kenya. Such researchers are known to be wealthy by local standards and would be perceived very negatively without assistance to those who provide help of any kind in research. In fact, one of the stresses under such conditions is coping with an often exaggerated misperception that all *wazungu* (white Europeans) are rich. Material compensation, even by many members of the general public, was therefore not only a personal value, but a cultural expectation as well. In sum, P. K. could participate with street children only in terms set forth by their cultural frame of reference about him. Following Michael Agar (1996), we believe that participant observation is a key ingredient in ethnography that "simply codes the assumption that the raw material of ethnographic research lies out there in the daily activities of the people you are interested in, and the only way to access those activities is to establish relationships with people, participate with them in what they do, and observe what is going on" (p. 31).

Unlike his Kenyan colleagues, P. K. as a *mzungu* participant observer, was able to travel to various sections of the city, as well as to Mombasa and other Kenyan cities where, as a stranger, he was able to experience encounters with street children who assumed he was a tourist. In Westlands, on the contrary, he struggled to "escape" from such a "distant" participatory role as "tourist," "missionary," or "social worker" in favor of what Clifford Geertz labels as an "experience near" participatory role of an "insider" participant observer (Geertz, 1983, p. 57). This was desirable since street children routinely act out stereotypical behaviors with friendly "outsiders" from whom resources are expected, sometimes on a regular basis, certainly well beyond our financial means in a long-term research project. With such outsiders, deception is often employed so as to obtain money or other material benefits. Consequently, during the first months of research, lying was frequently encountered by P. K. as his street boy informants in Westlands attempted to come to grips with his stated role as *mwalimu* (teacher) and writer of a book, one in which their own views and aspirations about street children would be featured. Still, while some boys did, on occasion, seem to appreciate our long-term research objectives, rapport came primarily from our financial ability to offer some employment to a few street boys who worked for us as interviewers, enumerators, or key informants. To other boys and girls, we gave small sums of money, more often food and clothing, in exchange for formal interviews and more formal participation in focus group discussions, which we organized separately for men, women, street boys, and street girls. Compensation was given for participants' loss of time at work, in scavenging for food or begging.

For most boys, as the years passed, P. K. became a "predictable" person, one who might give money for food this time if he had some or, if not, then perhaps the next time he would give something, a consistent pattern that was acceptable. His closest key informants routinely were given money, blankets, radios, and some of his personal items of clothing at the end of each summer research period. By the third year in Westlands, P. K. was able to "hang out" fairly unobtrusively while being ignored by most boys with whom he did not work closely. For some he was called *rafiki* (friend), for others *baba* (father) or *mzungu* (white person), but among his close informants "Phil." During the second summer of ethnographic work, P. K. was in a position to better evaluate the quality of his information. Street boys' stories by now corroborated (or not) accounts given to him by their comrades. Observation of actual behavior could be cross-checked with verbal statements sometimes themselves fabrications or ideals.

Unannounced "spot observations" (Munroe & Munroe, 1971) were invaluable, especially at night, to check whether events were unfolding as expected from informal discussions and participation held during the daytime. These also served to build a sense of "what happens" over the course of the daily and weekly period of social life. Information was cross-checked by asking similar questions to the same person on repeated occasions. Careful attention was paid to those instances when key informants verified, or did not, information provided by other boys. After some time, our closest informants made conscious attempts to "correct" errors of fact they noticed in conversations with P. K. Nevertheless, various instances of ambiguity remain in our material, especially for criminal activity and details of family history, both areas ripe for "identity" construction and fantasy.

P. K. attempted to systematically record his observations as field notes whenever time permitted. These field note observations were recorded in notebooks or on audiotapes. Initial observations were jotted down on a small notebook kept for this purpose. Such scrap notes (Sanjek, 1990, pp. 95–99) are useful mnemonic devices for reference when writing up or recording one's field notes. Included as field notes are such materials as published maps, news media stories, and other documents relevant to street children in Nairobi. Eventually, P. K. organized his materials primarily chronologically by year and by topics within each year. Specific street children who were followed over some years' duration are presented in this book as "Personal Profiles." Nevertheless, whatever classification and coding schemes go into one's field notes, they are highly personal and arbitrary according to the perceptions and interests of the ethnographer. Jean E. Jackson (1990), for example, writes "Field notes are liminal—betwixt and between—because they are between reality and thesis, between memory and publication" (p. 14).

In addition to participant observation and spot observations, our ethnographic methodology also involved interviews both formal and informal (see Agar, 1996, pp. 134–161). While interacting with street children, P. K. sometimes informally steered ongoing conversations in the direction of interest to him, sometimes unfortunately cutting off the flow of "natural conversation." Nevertheless, in time and with more patience, much was learned by listening to and participating in conversations among the children. Formal interviews were set up with specific children to explore special topics or to learn directly about their life stories. Such interviews conducted in places familiar to the children were useful occasions to get at social interpretations and experiences meaningful to the children. These ethnographic interviews were useful compliments to data collected more formally and around specific focused questions described in our focus group and survey research. Interviews were tape recorded.

During the summer of 1996, we were in a position to expand our ethnographic work to include street girls. This was made possible because the previous summer two street girls were fortuitously interviewed by P. K. at Westlands. He developed a good rapport with them after introductions by their street boy friends who were well-known to him. One of these girls served as a bridgehead into a street girl community where she lived in Jevanjee Gardens near the University of Nairobi. In 1996, as on previous occasions, students accompanied P. K. to Kenya. During that time, two female Bryn Mawr students participated in the daily life of a small number of Jevanjee Garden street girls. Nightlife, however, for these girls, especially survival sex, was only learned about through interviews from those in a position of full familiarity with such activities. Still, much about community life was learned by us not only through interviews but by participant observation, especially by the two Bryn Mawr students as they moved daily with street girls as they begged, socialized with one another, searched for food, washed clothes, sang songs, visited one another in jail, and observed how babies are integrated into the social life of street girls.

In our field research, we systematically sought to discover any social similarities and differences among street children by age, residence, and gender. In sum, ethnographic techniques served as an informative way to understand street children from our perspective of participant observation and interviews that emphasized their own voices and shared experiences arising from social life in the streets. Specifically, our methodology sought to provide a variety of opportunities for street children and others closely involved with their lives to speak directly to us about our understanding of their observed behavior and to express to us their own views on matters related to their lives. In chapter 5, we will present our focus group methodology and the results of our focus group interviews. These materials, which were organized by E. N. and P. K. in Kiswahili, were informative about aspirations voiced by the children and other matters pertaining to their position in Kenyan society. Street boys and street girls who participated in our focus group discussions were selected from among those whom we were involved with in our ethnographic research. Thus, they were familiar with us and at ease during the focus group interviews.

In the main, our ethnographic work, the focus group sessions, and our social survey to be described next, are together intended to be a contribution toward our objective of "testifying to other humanities" (Da Matta, 1994), in this case about the social world of street children, a way of life in which none of us has ever participated. For this reason we cannot speak directly as an insider, but we can (following Agar, 1996, p. 129) usefully, "paraphrase" street life by "giving an account" as informed by ethnographic and related techniques.

Our account in this book includes not only the social contexts and cultural understandings that shape the lives of street children in Nairobi. Once again, in following Agar, our analysis confirms his observation that much recent ethnographic research seeks to add "critical" questions, ones that sometimes transcend specific concerns of one's informants (1996, p. 27). Here we emphasize in the lives of street children patterns of social domination, hierarchy, and stigma that afflict their lives. While our overall account, we trust, would not be unfamiliar to street children, our interpretation of their exploitation is, as an epistemological issue, in the main derived from social science theory and comparative studies of street children globally. Our ethnographic and other techniques have highlighted our own theoretical concerns about them as much as anything we have been told directly by street children. While our account of their community and lives is ultimately part of our own worldview, it is not unreasonable. We are aware too, concerning the lives of street children as communicated to us, that in studying oppressive street cultures anywhere researchers rarely adequately "address the blood, sweat, and tears of real people suffering real oppressions in the imagined communities immediately sur-rounding our university campuses" (Bourgois, 1996, p. 254).

SURVEY

One of our key research techniques undertaken by C. S. was a social survey administered to four hundred street children and some of their family members, as well as NGO organizations, using prepared questions devised to elicit formal standardized responses. Social survey material in this book is based on data obtained from a baseline survey of 400 street children in Nairobi, 98 parents of the surveyed children, and 17 nongovernmental organizations (NGOs) working with street children in Nairobi. The study was done over a period of one and a half months between August and September 1993. The specific locations where participating street children were found and interviewed are shown in Table 2.1.

Although street children are a highly mobile group, there are certain places in the city where they tend to gather in large groups on a regular basis. The research team directed by C. S. identified such locations with the help of street children before and during the survey. Before the survey got underway, the research team searched throughout Nairobi in order to identify the specific streets and slums where street children are frequently found. During the survey, the children who had been interviewed were asked if they knew other places in town or in the slums where children like themselves could be found. A number of such places were identified through this process, and 27 of them were purposely selected for the study. Market places, shopping centers, and dumping grounds were found to be popular with street children because they scavenge for food and collect scrap metal, papers, and anything "valuable" they can get from these garbage heaps. The children in these locations were randomly selected for the interviews. The number of children interviewed in each location depended on the size of the group and the degree of cooperation from the children. Overall, we have sampled the most significant kinds of locations where street children are encountered in Nairobi. Although a deliberate effort was made to maintain gender balance in the sample, in reality there were more street boys than street girls found at any one location. This is what explains the gender disparity in the street children sample.

During the survey, six research assistants and the consultant in the selected locations in town and the slums administered structured questionnaires. The children were interviewed in the actual areas where they were found (see Table 2.1) and the interviews were conducted in Kiswahili. All the research assistants went to each area or location and did the interviews together before they could move to the next place. This strategy was intended to avoid the possibility of interviewing a child twice, which might have been the case if the research assistants were not moving in a group. The interviews covered a wide range of issues including demographic characteristics, occupational pursuits, major difficulties in street life, and views of their situation and aspirations for the future.

Table 2.1
Locations in Nairobi of Street Children Interviews

Locations	N	%
Uhuru Market	7	1.7
Mfangano Street	13	3.2
Muthurwa	15	3.8
Mathare Valley	15	3.8
Kariobangi Market	12	3.0
Dagoretti	21	5.3
Gikomba Market	16	4.0
Kenyatta Market	18	4.5
Burma Market	15	3.8
Gomongo	20	5.0
Racecourse Road	15	3.8
Moi Avenue	9	2.2
Forest Road Market	25	6.3
Kariokor Market	11	2.7
Ronald Ngala Street	19	4.7
Kenyatta Avenue (opposite NSSF bldg.)	12	3.0
Hurlingham Shopping Center	7	1.7
Uhuru Park	14	3.5
Kijabe Street	10	2.5
Soko Mjinga	21	5.2
Kimathi Street	9	2.2
Muindi Mbingu Street (near City Market)	15	3.9
River Road	10	2.5
Kibera	23	5.8
Ngara Market	19	4.7
Kenyatta Avenue (City Centre)	23	5.8
Around Ambassadeur Hotel	6	1.5
Total	400	100.0

As a cross-check on our survey materials, we interviewed a nonparticipating street boy who assisted us in other research about his assessment of our survey findings. While relaxing one evening with his key informant, Daniel, P. K. discussed with him a comprehensive, preliminary report of our social survey findings partially reported here. Daniel reported an almost complete agreement with our findings, adding some examples of his own to illustrate our conclusions. For example, he believes that begging is more common than the 46% figure in the report (based, of course, on what respondents "say" they do or believe). He offered one further clarification indicating that "older" boys smoked *bhangi* (marijuana) while younger ones only sniffed glue. The views of someone as familiar with street life as Daniel (see chapter 8, "Personal Profiles") and his strong agreement with our survey results, provided us with a

good "insider" cross-check, an example of the "cross-validation" objective constantly before us in a research population whose deception is often a survival
strategy.

We also interviewed some 98 parents of the surveyed children. The parents
were selected with the help of their own children on the streets. Each child who
was interviewed was asked if he/she could take the research team to his/her
family. Most of them were either unwilling or unable to do so for the following
reasons, each one significant in the lives of many children. Some of the children
could not take us to their homes because they came from far away and did not
want to leave their work for a long period of time. Some of the children come
from the surrounding communities outside Nairobi. Others, orphans particularly, said they had no families in town. Others had left school and gone to the
streets and were therefore afraid that if they went home, their parents would
punish them. There were also some children who told us that there was no point
going to their homes because their parents (mostly single mothers) were not
there because they always left home very early in the morning and returned late
in the evening. Most of these children had no idea what their parents were
doing or where they were going to every morning.

Nevertheless, despite these problems, those street children who were able
took us to their parents' homes in the residential areas and waited for us until
after the interviews when they accompanied us back to their places of work
where we had first met them. The places of residence for the families of these
children are shown in Table 2.2. Overwhelmingly, these children's families live
in the slums, a finding supporting a strong association between family, poverty,
and street children. Mathare Valley and Gomongo, where nearly half of our
families live, are among the poorest residential areas in Nairobi.

Most of the parents were interviewed in their own homes, although a small
minority was interviewed on the city streets where they were begging with their
children, these home visits making it possible for the research team to observe
the social, economic, and physical environment under which the families lived.
A few others were interviewed along the road within the estates where they
were hawking. In families where both parents were present only one parent was
interviewed. However, most of the surveyed parents were single mothers. The
interviews with parents covered a variety of issues ranging from their
socioeconomic backgrounds and original homes to the number of children they
had on the streets and their plans to keep them off the streets.

The last chapter of this book examines the experiences of some key NGOs
who are involved in the rehabilitation of street children. Seventeen NGOs were
selected and interviews held with the relevant officers in charge of programs for
street children. Structured questionnaires were administered to the officers in
the NGOs by C. S. herself. A list of the NGOs that were interviewed is
presented in Table 2.3.

Before NGOs were sampled for interviews, C. S. prepared a list of the NGOs
that have programs for children in difficult circumstances. There are many. Out

of these, those NGOs that deal primarily with street children were identified through a kind of snowball sampling in which the research team would ask an NGO person who had been interviewed to suggest another one engaged in similar activities. The NGOs were interviewed on a number of issues, including their program objectives, activities, the services provided to the children, their constraints, and what they consider to be the most effective strategy for rehabilitation. Interviews with NGOs were arranged in advance through appointments.

Social field survey is rarely without problems or challenges. Such work with street children poses special challenges. One of the difficulties experienced in the field was to get the street children to establish trust in the research team and to agree to be interviewed. This problem arose out of the children's suspicion of our motives as strangers. Since they did not know the research team or our purpose, their initial reaction was to avoid us. We got around this problem by explaining to the children our motives and emphasizing to them that we did not mean any harm. Their subsequent reaction toward us seemed to indicate that they believed us. The other reason for their reluctance to talk to us was that often they were at work and, therefore, did not want to spend too much time answering our questions, which would temporarily keep them away from looking for money. Many children expected to be given some money or food in return for giving us information. In some instances during the survey, interviews had to be interrupted every time someone passed by who looked like a potential benefactor so that the children could run to him/her to beg for money. They would always come back later to us to continue with the interviews. Another difficulty was how to verify the accuracy of some information the street children were giving us on some issues. There were some attempts primarily by the older children to misinform or to withhold or to manipulate information, depending on the issue. Such problems were overcome by probing and cross-checking. An integrated ethnographic and survey methodology is also beneficial in cross-checking information. Although the parents were generally cooperative, the main problem was how to get to their places of residence. Nearly all of them lived in the slums, and a lot of time was spent walking to their houses. Obviously, it would have been much more difficult without the help of the children. The NGOs, generally more familiar with research than are the children or their families, were also quite obliging.

In sum, our survey material focused on street children with the goal of providing a general profile of their lives through demographic information and the socioeconomic backgrounds of themselves and of their parents. Together, both sets of data revealed the realities of the children's world in terms of why they are on the street, their feelings about street life, what they do, why they do it, and the major difficulties they face in their work and family backgrounds. Our data also include the children's views and perspectives on their situation, assessment of their priority needs, the nature of the social support networks available to them, as well as their aspirations for and expectations of what programmatic action ought to be taken to create an alternative future for them. Our family interviews examined the socioeconomic backgrounds of the street children's families in order to determine the types of families that generate street children. It also dealt with what parent's thought needed to be done to keep their children off the streets. Our survey materials on children and families are reported in various chapters of this book.

In our survey, we also considered the experiences of key religious and nongovernmental organizations involved in the rehabilitation of street children. The main focus here is on the major program activities, the type of services provided, the program's effectiveness and output, an assessment of the constraints, and the implementers' perceptions and suggestions of what needs to be done differently in order to strengthen existing interventions for better results. Based on the experiences of the surveyed organizations and the analytical knowledge of the magnitude of the street children's problems and their real needs, we consider in our last chapter suggestions to improve NGOs' effectiveness in their often inspiring effort to ameliorate the situation and also to rehabilitate street children into useful members of society.

Ethnographic literary representation of "the other" is currently a significant issue in anthropology and related disciplines (Clifford & Marcus, 1986; Wolf, 1992; Behar & Gordon, 1995). We undertook writing about the social lives of street children from the perspective of epistemological assumptions mentioned in our discussion of our ethnographic methodology. Broadly, we frame our written materials around the assumption that there is a "real" world within which street children must find their way. In this sense, we assume "ethnographic realism" and seek to "get our facts" straight about the lives and circumstances pertaining to the children about whom we write. For this reason, for example, P. K. returned to Kenya when preparing ethnographic vignettes for our chapter introductions so as to visit specific places again in an effort to improve his capacity to write realistically about them. Places, events, and circumstances are not combined and are given here as ethnographic observations. Moreover, when discussing places, events, and specific children during our write-up, the three of us sought to do precise, factual descriptions. We are aware that "ethnographic realism" is considered problematic by some (Clifford & Marcus, 1986), such that we have thought about, for example, "ethnographic authority" in our writing. Clearly, we write here as "authorities," and we do so from a social science perspective. Nevertheless, in our view we have not excessively assumed this authoritative prerogative about the lives and aspirations of street children given our continuous effort to privilege the voices of street children in our research and in this text. The social constructionist alternative to ethnographic realism assumes social life is primarily invented, social practices are arbitrary, and theoretical generalizations are not possible (Marcus, 1994; Harris, 1994). In this view, social reality would be "socially constructed," for example, only through a dialogue between street children and the researchers. While dialogue and social construction are represented, we primarily write our materials from a theoretical perspective that wants to generalize that street children, while enjoying agency and not entirely passive victims of social circumstances, do, overall, suffer from social injustices. Thus we end our book with practical suggestions as to how we believe that street children can be eliminated as a social problem in Kenya and elsewhere. Margery Wolf (1992) takes a critical view of "postmodern" social constructionist assumptions preferring instead a view that accepts the theoretical and realist assumption that women universally have less social power than do men. Her feminist critique of postmodernism is compatible with our view that street children, especially girls, are powerless. No amount of dialogue between researchers and informants can eliminate this social fact. Wolf, however, believes that for certain audiences, ethnographic realism can be set aside in the forms of novels, short stories, and other fictional accounts. We too are not entirely hostile to multiple forms of representation in the social sciences.

In writing this collaborative book, we were able to reduce the outsider–insider gap between researcher and the "other" when extremes of differences separate them. C. S. and E. N., as indigenous writers, provided some cultural details here privileged by virtue of similar cultural understanding between researchers and Kenyan street children. In our discussions whenever disagreements over interpretation did arise, we did not rehearse our differences in these pages. Interestingly, there were no differences of opinion pertaining directly to street children, the subject of this book. P. K. and C. S., while sharing broad agreement on most issues of interpretation, did significantly disagree over the social power status of Kenyan women pertinent here to our analysis of gender roles and marriage and the family. Generally, P. K. holds Kenyan women to be more powerless than men to a greater degree than C. S., who herself tends to emphasize widespread female independence from men, female agency, and control over their own circumstances. There also was discussion about the suitability of publishing ethnographic information about the sexual practices and sexual orientations of street children. Sexual matters in Kenya are typically extremely private. In deference to this Kenyan belief, we agreed that such private information should not be published. What is relevant, however, is the striking degree of consensus the three of us discovered as our book developed over several years.

We have ended this chapter about our methodology with a discussion of our writing precisely because we value the postmodern critique of past unexamined assumptions about ethnographic realism in ethnography texts that permitted past excesses about detached "objectivity" in cultural description. Social science writing is, itself, significantly socially constructed and as such should be seen as an important part of the ethnographic research effort (Clifford & Marcus, 1986; Marcus, 1994). We hope that the reader will agree that our book takes into account the value of dialogue in research as well as recognition by us of individual variation among street children. The high degree to which their lives have been erroneously "socially constructed" in stereotypes held by outsiders will be evident too.

Table 2.2
Parental Place of Residence

Place of Residence	N	%
Kaloleni	4	4.1
Mathare Valley	28	28.6
Kibera	17	17.3
Majengo	3	3.1
Gomongo	20	20.4
Kawangware	4	4.1
Muthurwa	5	5.1
Makongeni	2	2.0
Korogocho	4	4.1
Huruma	3	3.1
Dandora	2	2.0
Mukuru Kayaba	1	1.0
Kanagemi	1	1.0
Gikomba/Gorofani	1	1.0
City Centre	3	3.1
Total	98	100.1

Table 2.3
Nongovernmental Organizations

NGOs (Nongovernmental Organizations)
Undugu Society of Kenya
Salvation Army
Mama Fatuma Goodwill Children's Home
St. Charles Lwanga Brothers
Kenya Children's Fund Trust (Dandora)
Sisters of Mercy (Mukuru Primary School)
Edelvale Homes (Embakasi)
Imani Maria House (Eastleigh)
PCEA Eastleigh Community Center
Don Bosco Boys Town
AIC Mashimoni (Kibera)
Thomas Barnardo Home (off Langata Road)
Tunza Dada Center (Pangani)
St. John's Catholic Church (Korogocho)
Dagoretti Corner Child Care Program
Kibagare Good News Center
Christian Children's Fund (Nairobi National Office)

Chapter 3

Cultural Contexts for Street Children: Family and Childhood

A mother in her late 20s hurried along a deserted dirt road hoping that she would reach the primary school in time. She wore a fashionable, tight-fitting, blue skirt and matching low heels appropriate for her office job as a secretary for which she would be late today. Like many other mothers of her age and social class, this one was nervously anticipating a place for her child at one of the city's better schools, a place thought necessary by urban parents for the future success of their children. In a nation where "retirement benefits" are not routine, most Kenyan parents think of their children, not only with feelings of love but also in terms of significant future resources for help in their old age. As the mother continued along the road, the rising sun shone against the green and white mosque, an imposing backdrop for this woman as she half-consciously sidestepped hens and urinating goats in this city of significant urban agriculture. Her destination, the school, stood near the Mama Ngina Kenyatta Children's Home and the YMCA Hostels. Once at the school to her relief, as she later confided to me, she found the queue was not yet too long even though many women had already arrived. All of the many mothers and the few fathers present hoped to be called back for an interview on another day, something assured to them if they were to receive an application form today. Like many women in the queue, this mother, my informant, is unmarried; therefore, she has the sole economic responsibility for her child, for whom she receives little help from the father even though the father is wealthy. Also, the father is married, a station responsible for his cautious, secretive acknowledgment of his paternity, expressed only through occasional gifts. The mother carries with her a small "chai" (bribe) in case the teacher in charge requests a bribe, not unlikely since the teachers' union that very day was on the brink of a national strike because of pitifully low teachers' salaries. Teachers too, she realized, are parents and not only have their own children to care for, but those of other relatives as well. As in the past, Kenyans continue to value extended family ties and obligations. (Kilbride field notes, 1996)

Bribery is, in fact, now endemic throughout the society. Kinsmen alone can no longer be counted on to help out in a pinch. An "anti-corruption authority" committee was established in 1998 to hear and prosecute public complaints, although the chairman, soon after his appointment, was removed for investigating "higher-ups." Many doubt his ability to curb bribes, so widespread for even routine services such as obtaining a passport, visiting a friend in jail, obtaining water from the Nairobi city council, getting a place/job in government agencies or in schools of all kinds, and so on. Frequently foreign donors and local benefactors have sometimes given money and materials targeted for street children only to have their donations "eaten" by "the wrong hands." In one case known to the authors, an "outside" international donor gave a Land Rover intended for use by a Nairobi child welfare agency, but it ended up in the Uasin Gishu grain belt hundreds of kilometers away from Nairobi ferrying crops at harvest for a member of the agency.

In the past, bribery for education, as it occurred in the case described, was rare because education was free. Presently, however, forces of unregulated capitalism have taken over all sectors of Kenyan society, including education. These days, university students are regularly poised for strikes against the policies of the International Monetary Fund and the World Bank because of their doctrinaire imposition of "free market" standards on Kenya so that the ability to pay school fees, more than academic merit, increasingly serves as a means to select and retain students in public universities.

Street children can be understood as one consequence of the rising culture of capitalism and the declining significance of African indigenous values, under which children were reared in strong family kinship units. In such extended families both fathers and mothers were indispensable for the social and spiritual development of children. Today, although many indigenous values are widely practiced in some form or another, it is the historically declining cultural significance of the responsible father's role as family "provider" in the lives of his children that needs to be highlighted here. The absent father, often gone because of alcoholism or desertion, is related to the continuing and growing presence of street children in Kenya. Economic poverty, rural to urban migration involving men more than women, and the decline of circumstances favorable to the extended family are all interrelated factors in the unavailability of fathers for many children.

INDIGENOUS FAMILY VALUES

We turn now to an overview of key cultural elements behind the family structure widespread in indigenous Kenyan communities. These family values and practices are by no means a thing of the past but are still widely practiced, particularly in rural areas, and are often valued, especially by older Kenyans, as ideals (Kilbride & Kilbride, 1990; Adepoju, 1997; Weisner, Bradley, & Kilbride, 1997; Suda, 1999; Parkin & Nyamwaya, 1987; and Swadener, Kabiru, & Njenga, 1996).   The following family materials have been specifically selected to be contrasted with present circumstances, in which numerous street children and other categories of children live in conditions of physical and economic abuse and are exploited as laborers.   While the past was certainly not without imperfections, especially in widespread gender inequality and female circumcision in some societies, those conditions were by no means ubiquitous, and women did have considerable economic power compared to the present (Nasimiyu, 1997).

In addition to setting a historical context in which the street children problem emerged as indigenous family values declined, we intend that the material in this chapter be read for possible areas of family support that might be revitalized so as to assist street children who now live outside regular family exchanges and assistance.   We return to this subject in our last chapter where we discuss a cultural model emphasizing Kenyan-derived indigenous family values for addressing the street children problem in Kenya.

Most Kenyans today generally are raised in the context of large households and joint families.   Maria Cattell (1997) writing about the Samia, describes a pattern common today throughout rural areas in Kenya.   She observes about the past and the continuing persistence of family ties into the present, "Intergenerational relationships were played out over lifetimes lived in clearly defined spaces, where family caregivers were likely to be readily available . . . now many families have members who live in other rural areas in Kenya, in cities, and abroad" (p. 162).   Cattell notes also that current geographically dispersed extended families permit family members to participate in local and urban wage labor economies.

Mothers are usually assisted in the care of their infants and toddlers by abundant household members including young caretakers who care for a younger sibling.   For this reason, a special bond often prevails between a child caretaker and her sibling "follower" in the birth order.   If no girl is available, a boy can also be a caretaker.   Parents, in the main, desire to have both boys and girls.   Boys are valued in those Kenyan ethnic societies (the majority) where descent is traced through males (patrilineal descent), who then inherit land while girls do not.   In a patrilineal, patrilocal society, kinship is determined through the father's line, and at marriage a woman leaves her own kin group and goes to live with her husband's kin group.   Often this involves a move over some distance.   Only sons in a partilineal society inherit land from their families whereas the families of girls, however, receive gifts from their future in-laws on the occasion of their marriage into the husband's family, a custom known as bridewealth payment.   Although women today may own land, bridewealth payment is still common and could assume a high profile while signifying prestige in cases such as those involving highly educated women.

BRIDEWEALTH

In Kenya, extended family households and family ties beyond the household are still much more prevalent than nuclear family units made up of husband, wife, and their children. For this reason, most marriages are really between extended families, not merely between two individuals as in the West. Bridewealth serves to cement family relations and also represents a sign of value for a newly married woman who leaves behind valuables for her natal family after leaving home to join her husband. Of course, this system also highlights a strong pro-natal emphasis as the bride is expected to have children, all of whom will "belong" to her husband and his family. In indigenous, agrarian communities, children are sources of wealth as potential contributors to the household workforce. Today, bridewealth payment is still widely practiced, even in cases involving university women, many of whom command very high brideprices that constitute an exchange for investments in their education provided by their family members since childhood (Hakansson, 1988).

In patrilineal families such as the Abaluyia, among whom bridewealth is exchanged, the maternal brother has a special tie to the sister who provided him with the brideprice for his own marriage. In fact, bridewealth is better referred to as "progeny price" since it bestows to a man and his natal family the rights of "ownership" of the children produced by the marriage. This practice occurs where marriage predominantly links families rather than individuals. Typically, the husband's family gives to the wife's family material items such as cattle, blankets, and money in exchange for the rights to the children the wife will produce in the marriage. If no children are produced, the husband's family has the option of requesting the return of the bridewealth given or, in some communities, the husband marries the sister of the childless wife. Because a woman has the potential to bring in bridewealth today, an illegitimate daughter may be more readily accepted by her mother's future husband than would a son for whom land, now in decreasing supply, is needed. Street girls, therefore, potentially have "kinship capital" in current marriage practices in Kenya should they ever be rehabilitated into families as we propose in the last chapter.

SIBLING CARETAKING

Extended families in Kenya can be thought of as "sibling caretaking societies" where reciprocal family ties, especially sibling ones, serve to assist individuals when in need (Weisner, 1982). We have seen how brideprice payment practices serve to cement ties between brothers and sisters. Same sex siblings are also important as for example in age hierarchies where older siblings care for younger ones, frequently acting as child nurses to them. One Kenyan man recalls his experience as an *ayah* (child nurse) as follows:

I was not yet four years old when my sister was born. I had got used to sleeping away from my mother's care, having been so long with my uncle. On my return, together with other male youngsters of very nearly the same age, I began to sleep in my grandfather's hut. [The girls of this age also would sleep away from their parents' homes and at some grandmother's house.] Because there was no older sister in the family, and my mother had gone off to work in the *shamba* (farm) every day, it wasn't long before I was obliged, though still a very young child myself, to become the day-to-day nurse for my baby sister. We would attend to our babies only when they cried excessively. Then we would sing lullabies to make them go to sleep quickly, hurriedly feed them, or perhaps tie them, still crying, on our backs and continue playing. (Lijembe, 1967, p. 4)

Included as socializing agents are older brothers and sisters, some of whom have been sibling caregivers. Thomas Weisner (1982), writing on the general topic of sibling interdependence and child caregiving, described the sharing of parental care as part of a "shared functioning family system and an affiliative rather than egoistic individualistic style of achievement and competence" (p. 316). Thus, fostering may be viewed in the context of adult interdependence, of which caregiving by children, who are most frequently 7–14 years of age, is an integral part. Weisner (1987) believes that sibling care is most prevalent in situations in which "there are large, co-resident families, customs encouraging fosterage, adoption, and exchange of children between households, higher fertility, and low use of birth control" (p. 246). Such conditions allow for more available household helpers. In his own fieldwork in Kenya among the Abaluyia, who typify this kind of shared care system, Weisner found that 74% of the 70 mothers he interviewed reported that, as children, they had done sibling care either in their natal homes or in the homes of relatives. Also, 54% of the mothers reported that relatives or hired maids helped in their childhood homes (Weisner, 1987, p. 261).

FOSTERING

Sibling interdependence is a significant feature underlying a widespread pattern of fostering throughout Kenya (Kilbride & Kilbride, 1994). An assistant to the director of social services at Nangina Hospital Social Services in western Kenya described the following four occasions for fostering in Samia location in western Kenya from most to least common (see Kilbride & Kilbride, p. 319).

1. A child born out of wedlock will live with his or her mother's parents, usually permanently.
2. At the death of one or both parents, a child may move to live with a relative (uncle, aunt, etc.) after the funeral.
3. A child is sent to a "more prosperous" relative but will visit his or her parents regularly and will eventually return to live with them.
4. If living alone, one can request a child from a sister to alleviate loneliness or to live

in the house while the resident is away at work, on night duty, or periodically absent.

From her own experience in her work, Mrs. Olalle sees fostering, for one or another of the aforementioned reasons, occurring commonly. She estimates that about one half of the children in her community are fostered. The Samia attach no stigma to being a foster child. Mrs. Olalle also pointed out that, among the Samia, the age at which fostering occurs varies in terms of who is fostered and the specific circumstances surrounding the fostering event. Children from infancy on up are fostered by grandparents; children are fostered to a wealthy relative from 5 years or older (school age); in cases of the death of a parent, children from infancy to age 18 are fostered. To alleviate loneliness, children 10 years or older are fostered. Both boys and girls may be fostered to relatives. Children with disabilities are not fostered traditionally for fear that they may be mistreated, but instead are "spoiled" at home. Overall, the most common recipients of foster children are grandparents, wealthy relatives, and childless relatives. We will return to the subject of fostering in the last chapter, where we will propose ways that fostering can be thought about as a culturally appropriate channel for the rehabilitation of street children.

GRANDPARENTS

Grandparents are often resources for child fostering. We learn, for example, from H. Aswani (1972), concerning one large ethnic group that is typical, that because old women love to please children, Abanyore literature is composed of many folk tales. "Old women . . . would sit down by the fireside and tell as many stories as they could think of before the children became sleepy" (p. 1). Stories told to children were concerned with pending adolescent life and were for entertainment. They discussed the domestic life of married women and men. Such stories were told to both adolescent and adult audiences. "They were meant to warn both boys and girls of what they were to expect of their respective partners when they married. . . . The stories were also meant to teach the young men how to behave in crises which might arise in family life" (Aswani, p. 2). Idealized themes in these stories stressed morals concerning, for example, sincere love, caution, and the avoidance of pride and laziness.

It was not believed that grandparents should ideally assume total economic support for grandchildren, but there is idealized support for the notion that grandparents are and should be involved in "asymmetrical" exchanges with grandchildren. Grandparents should ideally "give" presents, food, and goodwill (traditionally grandchildren sometimes sleep at the house of grandparents, where they can be "spoiled"). The major "provider" role was that of the father. Because of increased marginalization of the indigenous nonmonetary economy, many fathers are now living away from their children in search of money.

Childcare responsibility is falling too often on the shoulders of caring grandparents. To refuse a grandchild is, in Kenya, to go against both convention and psychological sentiment.

Today many grandparents are quite heavily burdened by caring for their daughter's child, the one most frequently left behind when she marries. Throughout Kenya in the recent agrarian past, children of both sexes served as a bulwark for assistance in one's old age and a source of agricultural labor in the present. Moreover, children symbolized economic success of the family unit, blessings from providence, and social power. Not infrequently a man welcomed and adopted his children born before his marriage. In some societies fertility was so strongly emphasized that a young girl could increase her chance of marriage by becoming pregnant (Wagner, 1949; 1956). Currently, overburdened grandparents expressed their view that children are, on the whole, no longer as highly valued as previously by their fathers in part because of monetary expenses associated, for example, with schooling and clothing (Kilbride & Kilbride, 1990, 1997). Kenya's demographic crisis has impacted directly on grandparents (Bradley, 1997, pp. 240–242). The following case is not unusual in rural Kenya where large numbers of homes are still intergenerational and as such have resident grandchildren. "This fifty-two-year old man lives with his wife, six sons, and a daughter. Two other sons and two other daughters have married and live elsewhere, but one daughter-in-law lives at his home with her three children. Two children of the other daughters-in-law also live with them. He has, however, a total of seven grandchildren living with him, because each of the two daughters who have married out left behind a child she gave birth to before her marriage. These two grandsons, who call him father, were not accepted by their mothers' husbands. . . . It should be noted that these grandparents still have seven of their own children living with them" (Kilbride & Kilbride, 1997, p. 216).

A growing result of HIV infection in Kenya today is the increased burden and stress for the extended family, especially grandparents, who are left to care for AIDS orphans. In the past, the extended family system provided an effective safety net for the small number of orphans in the family and community. This is because children did not belong to the nuclear family into which they had been born, but to the whole clan, which also had the responsibility of providing care and support to the needy (Mukoyogo & Williams, 1993). However, a study by Paul Saoke and Roselyn Mutemi (1994, p. 9) indicates that orphans in Kenya find it increasingly difficult to be accepted and supported within the extended family network even though the household heavily depends on their labor. The study further reveals that most orphans cite a series of problems, including the fact that they eat less and last and are often more prone to malnutrition and infections and less likely to receive health care than other children. With all areas of Kenya showing an upward trend in HIV prevalence rates, many grandparents will suffer the burden of caring for young children and growing numbers of households will be headed by children in their early teens because relatives are either unwilling or unable to provide care and support that children need for their social and emotional development. HIV/AIDS and lack of support are major factors in the increasing number of street children in Kenya today. Nevertheless, despite current hardships experienced by grandparents who have been pressed into taking on provider roles, we will consider in our last chapter how a revitalized fostering program, especially by grandparents, should be considered as a cultural mechanism to assist street children to leave the streets or to prevent them from going there in the first place.

POLYGYNY

In Kenya, polygyny, although illegal today except for Muslims and in customary law, is a common practice even though many Christian churches disallow the custom. Polygyny is the marriage practice in which a spouse is married to more than one person at a time. When the man has multiple spouses, the term "polygyny" is used. Polyandry is used when a woman has multiple spouses. Joseph Ssennyonga (1997) reports, "Polygyny is prevalent in the Lake Victoria Basin. For example, a 1984 survey shows that the percentages of currently married women in polygynous unions are thirty-eight, forty-seven, and forty-one for Kisumu, Siaya, and South Nyanza districts, respectively. A 1987 survey on Rusinga Island provides higher ratios: 34 percent of the married men and 56 percent of the women are living in polygynous unions" (p. 269).

Among the Abaluyia, as another example, polygyny has been, and continues to be, a cultural ideal. Nevertheless, the majority of families are monogamous, as is usually the case where polygyny is the ideal. In a social survey, only between 5% and 10% of households were polygynous (Kilbride & Kilbride, 1990). Ideally throughout Kenya, a polygynous man should be wealthy, having enough land and economic resources to support his wives and children, as well as to provide help to extended family members. At the same time, the agricultural work provided by his wives and their children should serve to increase the wealth of the family and their power and prestige in the community. The large family also provides protection against perceived, hostile outsiders. Today, however, as a result of a declining significance of cultural sanctions that once regulated the practice of polygyny and a greater reliance on a monetary economy, an increasing number of men who lack the monetary resources are, unfortunately, polygynous. This frequently results in harsh circumstances for their wives, many of whom depend on their husbands for income, and children, for whom insufficient funds hinder their lives.

Women in some Kenya communities are often in support of polygyny under the right circumstances. A Catholic nun and a Kenyan nurse undertook a survey in western Kenya. G. Lwanga (n.d.) reports the following concerning her discussions of polygyny with 27 Samia women living in a remote rural area of western Kenya. Many Samia women felt that polygyny can be a happy and beneficial experience if the co-wives cooperate with one another. They caution, however, that this is not likely to happen unless the husband allows the senior wife the chance to look for a second wife for her husband. She often chooses a relative or the daughter of another family of whom she approves. If he should require a third wife, these two wives would then be informed so that they could help to look for someone with whom they would wish to share their lives and work. Women felt that the most common reason a wife would advise her husband to take another wife was that he was a rich man with lots of cattle and land, too much for one wife to handle alone. Out of the 27 women, 25 considered polygyny to be better than monogamy. Other studies in Kenya also have suggested that traditional (usually rural, uneducated) women view polygyny more positively than their educated counterparts.

Studying another Kenyan society, the Kipsigis, Mulder (1992) found that married women have strong views concerning polygyny that are generally positive. Seventy-six percent of the women in her survey viewed polygyny favorably. In general, she found that co-wife relations were not full of tension, nor did polygynously married women suffer reproductive costs. Neither women nor their parents expressed antipathy toward polygyny (Mulder, p. 179). Very much present in Kenya at this time is a consciousness of the importance of having fathers for children, although with a rise in divorce and marginalization of polygyny, an indigenous value, many single women now assume sole caretaking responsibilities. This can be a strain for many such women. Whatever the value orientation is toward polygyny, the reality is that throughout Kenya most men, nevertheless, turn out to be monogamous. Moreover, educated women are usually opposed to polygyny as an ideal, especially the unregulated "secret" polygyny that prevails today (Kilbride, 1994).

In general, our interviews revealed that Kenyans have both positive and negative memories about growing up in polygynous homes. Although jealousy and conflict were present, especially between co-wives concerning economic injustices, this was less likely to be the case when the polygynous home was a wealthy one. Importantly, in keeping with traditional values, whether talking about the past or the present, more positive impressions about life in a polygynous home as parents or as children were given if the family was rich. The following case of a man we shall call Joseph will illustrate this pattern. Joseph is actually now wealthy because he has judiciously managed his marriages to maximize the monetary wealth potential of what is a "polygynous family business." Joseph is a vibrant, energetic man in his late fifties. He speaks with enthusiastic optimism about his "plans" to educate his children. His first wife is from Uganda. She lives on a 58-acre farm near Eldoret and is responsible for producing food for her family, including subsequent co-wives of hers married by Joseph. He now resides in a small town not far from his first wife's farm on a three-acre plot with his other two wives and some of their children. Joseph's second wife runs a *duka* (general store) next to her son's tailor shop. A third wife operates a nursery school there. The family business also has a dispensary employing a nurse and a midwife. Behind the business buildings are several residential cement structures. These are prosperous homes separately occupied by his two wives and their children.

Joseph has twenty-three children, some of whom work "in the business" (one daughter, for example, acquired skills as a seamstress). The homes usually contain one or another of his school-age children, home for holidays or from nearby schools. His children also number at least one educated at the university level. Joseph's daughter and her stepbrother run the tailor shop. They report some conflict at home but nothing one would not expect in any marriage, be it monogamous or polygamous. They stated that Joseph does have some problems satisfying all of his children's needs but also observed that he "managed" his home well. Each child, for example, was consciously placed by Joseph with a stepmother to minimize conflict. All the children are required to work on the farm maintained by the senior wife.

There is a less favorable case of polygyny than Joseph's family, a case of growing up in a polygynous home by a man in his mid-20s, here called Robert. His father has four wives but, unfortunately, limited economic means. He has 31 children thus far, the youngest being less than one year old. Also, Robert's mother is not in a very favorable position economically or in terms of respect; she is his father's second wife. In Robert's early childhood, his father had only two wives, both of whom Robert called "mother." It was not until he was seven years old that he began to question his status. When he was eight years old, he recollects going to school for a while with the sons of the first wife. It was not a pleasant memory: his stepbrothers beat him, made him carry their books to and from school, and forced him to get money from his mother to give to them for their own lunches. He finally refused to go to that school, which was 10 kilometers away, so he was transferred to a school near his home. After fourth grade, he states that he was forced to go to another primary school near the home of the fourth wife. While living at her house, which is 15 miles from the home of his mother and the other two wives who all share the same compound, Robert complains that he was forced to do many household chores, including cooking, cleaning, and tending livestock. At times he went without food from breakfast until dinner. He also disliked the fact that when he had friends over to visit, his stepmother would say that he wasn't living in the home of his mother. "It made me feel that I was born somewhere else but was now under the control of another person" (Kilbride & Kilbride, 1990, p. 208).

Robert now understands that there are some advantages to polygyny, such as sharing the workload, helping to care for other family members when they or their children are sick, and preventing childlessness and thus gaining immortality through one's children. Nevertheless, the disadvantages he has experienced personally make him unfavorable to polygyny and what he believes to be its many problems of jealousy and conflict over insufficient resources for food, clothing, and education.   He remembers that during times of food shortage, his mother and her co-wives looked after only their own children with no sharing among co-wives.   When food and money for school fees were in short supply, Robert's father tended to "disappear" until the worst was over.   In Robert's case, we see one major problem of modern-day polygyny in that his father did not fit the traditional ideal of being wealthy enough to be a polygynist, at least on the scale that he practiced it.   Robert maintains that his own reaction to polygyny is to a great extent the result of a lack of sufficient monetary resources by his father, who irresponsibly married more wives than he could economically support.

CURRENT STATUS OF POLYGYNY

The fate of polygyny in Africa is very much caught up in the processes of moral and economic change.   The churches vary considerably in terms of overt condemnation of polygyny, with the mainstream churches being predominantly opposed and many independent churches being favorable toward polygyny. Community sanctions traditionally at work in regulating polygyny have changed as well, and elders and other traditional moral leaders have lost the authority they had in the past, when practices like polygyny were closely monitored.   One finds in Kenya today, many men, who traditionally would not have been considered acceptable as polygynists in terms of their economic resources, practicing polygyny because community sanctions no longer operate with the same degree of salience as in the past.   As traditions change and the modern economy and moral order impose themselves more and more into the everyday lives of people, polygyny increasingly takes on a negative ambiance.   Many highly educated men in modernizing circumstances, in fact, relate much of the current female opposition to polygyny to the current irresponsible practice of this custom.   Surprisingly, a few educated women are not hostile to polygyny. In our last chapter we will consider to what extent, if any, a "reinvented" polygynous tradition may serve to alleviate to some extent the street children problem, itself of recent historical origin beginning at a time when the indigenous practice of polygyny began to deteriorate into its present marginalized and often stigmatized, unregulated but widespread form.

INITIATION RITUALS

Puberty is marked in many societies by initiation rites such as male circumcision or female clitoridectomy.   Circumcision serves to tie together young males into a common social group who will bond for life as they make the transition from childhood to manhood.   Among the Bukusu, for example, circumcision ceremonies are held every four years.   Young initiates of twelve or thirteen years of age are carried on the shoulders of their male and female relatives in celebration of their new public identity. It is considered shameful and cowardly to express pain while being publicly circumcised. Bukusu men from all walks of life and from all over the world are said to make efforts to return to Bukusu land to witness the circumcision of their relatives.

There are in Kenya many societies that do not circumcise their men, such as the Luo, Kenya's second largest ethnic group. Most ethnic groups do not practice clitoridectomy although it is found among the Abagusii, Pokot, Kikuyu, and a few other societies. Unlike male circumcision, this practice is very controversial and the subject of considerable national and international debate even when it is undertaken with modern medical precautions. Many folk explanations such as the control of female sexuality or the enhancement of female solidarity are now largely discredited in contemporary Kenya. On the whole, initiation ceremonies provide a strong basis for peer solidarity. Like sleeping arrangements, they also serve to detach the child, especially a boy, from his family relations, particularly with his mother. At the same time, sleeping arrangements foster a culturally appropriate sense for moving beyond the household during adolescence to seek meaningful relationships elsewhere. Thus, sleeping on the streets with other street boys can be seen, to some extent, as a distorted means for enhanced mobility outside the household, especially given that peer relationships are so strongly emphasized among boys on the streets. For street girls, the situation is more problematic, as we shall see.

HOME LIFE AND SLEEPING ARRANGEMENTS

Street children believe that sleeping inside, even in a slum house, as compared to outside, provides better protection from the police, thieves, and cold and rainy weather. The idea, however, of sleeping apart from parents during adolescence or in the company of one's peers is not foreign to Kenyan cultural norms. This custom, along with others pertaining to sleeping, is practiced in one form or another, most predominantly in the rural areas. Today's sleeping customs are derived with modification from indigenous settlement patterns, household arrangements, and family cultural values under changing circumstances.

Exclusively in the past and still common today among some Kenyan societies are indigenous houses of wattle and daub, for example, which were built within a fenced enclosure for each large family. Within the enclosure, age and gender distinctions served to define where and with whom each person would sleep at night. Husbands, especially polygynous ones, slept separately from their wives, and each wife had her own hut where she slept with her children. The father-husband had his own hut but visited his wives' homes for meals and visitations, ideally on a rotating basis. Children slept within family compounds but usually apart from their fathers and, as they grew older, their mothers as well. Boys and girls slept in separate "bachelor" homes often under the watchful gaze of a grandmother. Grandparents slept in their own room or in a separate hut for each grandparent.

When approaching adolescence, boys and girls slept apart, not infrequently, in separate sleeping areas, the details varying somewhat by ethnic group. Girls, at times, would visit the boys' places for romantic encounters. Frequently, the girl's hut was a place where an "old grandmother" would supervise young girls and entertain them with stories and advice about life skills needed for social success. Storytelling was also a common form of entertainment in the family compound before going to bed (see Ominde, 1952).

Children did not sleep "as a family" nor even in the same hut or compound for long periods of time. Typically, children slept with a variety of relatives and friends during childhood and adolescence. The sense of having one's "own bedroom" ended in early childhood after weaning, when the child no longer slept exclusively in the same bed or bedroom with his/her mother. Fostering of children also encouraged shifts of residence contributing to the notion that mobility was expected during childhood. In many societies in Kenya, circumcision rites and other rituals served to bind adolescent boys, and sometimes girls, into strong peer groups, ones that bound children together apart from their family ties and domestic spaces (see Kenyatta, 1965). The idea of "sleeping for pleasure" was not emphasized. Sleeping routines varied by the seasons and by social occasions. People generally went to bed earlier during the rainy season compared to the dry, for instance, and slept infrequently during funerals and mourning ceremonies, which usually lasted for three or four days, depending on the sex and social status of the deceased.

Beds, pillows, and mattresses have largely replaced cowhides and sleeping mats nowadays. Men rarely rise in the middle of the night to inspect by moonlight their compound for footprints of thieves or other unwelcome visitors. Schoolwork, radio, and television have largely replaced grandmothers' stories as significant bedtime events. Still, the parent and grandparent generations of current street children, coming as they do from poor and often rural backgrounds, are not unfamiliar with the sleeping practices described here. Thus, the idea of their adolescent children sleeping away from home, without a special bedroom and in somewhat unpleasurable conditions would not be thought of, in and of itself, as unusual either for themselves or for their children.

CHILD ABUSE

Some writers suggest that street children in Kenya represent an example of child abuse (Suda, 1997). Indeed modern Kenyan society, when compared to its indigenous past, has witnessed a dramatic increase in social circumstances unfavorable to children. M. Bwibo (1982), a Kenyan pediatrician, states that "recent figures show that in 1980/81, 21 children with battered child syndrome were admitted to Kenyatta National Hospital of whom 5 died" (p. 11). Of significance to our present discussion, Bwibo notes that victims of child abuse frequently included (1) "The babies of single mothers thrown along the road, dropped in pit latrines or dustbins" and (2) "the babies whose hands are burnt because they stole money from the homes" (p. 11). His cases included male and female abusers who, apart from the parents, included stepparents and child caretakers.

Common forms of child abuse in Kenya involve getting rid of an unwanted infant or child by abandonment and attempted or actual infanticide. Both boys and girls are at risk and the "pit latrine" is a common location for disposal of unwanted children (Kilbride, 1991). Press reports of child torture, burning, scalding, battering, prolonged confinement, and the like are not uncommon (Kilbride & Kilbride, 1990). Frequent editorials are encountered with such titles as "Our Sad Problem of Battered Children" and "State Urged to Tighten Laws on Child Abuse." While many street children are arguably not abused in the strict sense of the term, as in the battered child syndrome, we feel that our material clearly shows that they suffer regular abuse, perhaps beginning in their families, but later meted out to them in a variety of extrafamilial contexts involving the police, respective members of the public in pursuit of sexual gratification, and a tolerance for the very condition of their homelessness and marginal social status, a situation considered unbelievable by many rural residents who remember a much better time in the past. The roots of child abuse in Kenya require a consideration of colonial history.

COLONIALISM

Colonial policies throughout Africa frequently had a disruptive impact on families and children. Families were split because of migration to cities by men in search of work to pay taxes, in Kenya known as the "hut tax" (Kilbride & Kilbride, 1990). Children themselves were often exploited on plantations and in factories by those in search of economic profit. In Zimbabwe, for instance, there are currently street children on Harare's streets (Bourdillon, 1991). Street children in numbers, however, have been present in Zimbabwe since World War I. Beverly Grier (1996) argues that street children in Zimbabwe, throughout the colonial era from the 1920s through the 1950s, were a result of land dispossession, overstretched resources, growing rural poverty, and low wages. In sum, they were due to dislocations caused by the colonial political economy. Among these colonial policies was the introduction of child labor. Gleaning from available colonial documents, Grier described 10 to 14 year-old children who came into the towns, mines, and other industrial centers of southern Rhodesia to work as casual porterages (laborers) and for businesses. Many such children lived on their own in the streets. There were fewer girls on the streets than boys, but girls under fourteen were numbered among prostitutes in the colonial, dislocated economy, in which they serviced a largely male workforce. Grier notes, moreover, that children worked on white-owned farms where harsh working conditions often caused them to run away, often to the streets. While Grier describes the unfavorable circumstances resulting from a colonial, political economy, she also feels that many children were running away from sometimes-oppressive family circumstances often characterized by authoritarian family structures. On the whole, Zimbabwean street children, presently and in the past, are best understood as exercising their agency in resistance to unfavorable circumstances.

Kenya's colonial past also involved oppressive labor practices for children. D. Kayongo-Male and P. Walji (1984) have documented the historical story of children at work in Kenya. They document conditions of forced child labor, rapes of women and girls, and harsh working conditions on plantations and in factories. They write, for example, "Whenever the men were scarce because of migration, conscription into military service or detention, women and children helped fill the labor gap. . . . In 1924 there was a particularly acute shortage of labor, especially in the coffee districts. . . . In 1925 there were 11, 315 children at work, mostly in tea and coffee picking. Moreover, there were others under ten years of age who were hired by railway and ballast contractors for heavy fuel and stonecutting tasks"(p. 41). Kayongo-Male and Walji further report that there were about 5,500 children working on the ten estates at Kericho and Limuru every year with many others at work on sisal, coffee, and pyrethrum estates. Thousands of children still work in Kenya's plantations.

Chapter 4

Nairobi: A City of Contrasts

It was clear that many residents of Korogocho were not used to seeing a "mzungu," like me, certainly not up close. This became apparent as I walked ahead of a social activist priest who had invited me to see his programs for street children. About thirty children curiously rushed from all directions forward to feel my arms (hairy and white) while shouting habari gani, mzungu (how are you, white man). It is, in fact, likely that few Korogocho residents have ever visited Nairobi's central business district so as to observe white people up close in cars or on foot. This lack of exposure to affluent Kenyans and visitors is not unexpected in a community of low-income migrant workers with low educational levels. Later, while walking out of Korogocho on the same road, I reflected on the priest's comments about how he considered Korogocho as a "feeder" community for street children in Nairobi. This occurred later after I had been escorted by the tall, gregarious priest–social worker through the community and into some homes, a feat requiring acrobatic-like maneuvers to avoid ubiquitous excrement and urine-stained pools of water resulting from a scarcity of toilets. A fee of one shilling is sometimes charged to use fortunate neighbors' toilet services. This small amount can be a prohibitive fee for many residents. While listening to the priest, I observed some drunken men staggering along the road talking to no one in particular. Suddenly, as father raised his arms in making an emphatic comment, a young man sprinted by and grabbed his watch from his wrist. Without breaking stride, the thief disappeared into the mass of late afternoon pedestrians, many of whom were heading home to Korogocho from their unskilled jobs in Nairobi or from their failed attempts to find employment. (Kilbride field notes, 1994)

COMMUNITY VARIATION

Stretched out toward the horizon as far as the eye can see, standing astride both sides of the narrow road, are countless stalls stocked with a bewildering variety of items of food and other necessities. This open market grades rather abruptly into the slums of Korogocho, a slum like others in Nairobi that give rise to street children from conditions of abject poverty and social decay. With a population density of about 4,800 per square kilometer, over 100,000 people reside here. The visitor is struck immediately by a sense of demographic thickness and an immensity of geographical scale as the eye extends in all directions in a distant vista of people, houses, and commercial stalls.

One immediately encounters the vastness of human and material presence upon entering Korogocho, beginning with the vegetable and fruit stalls. These were filled with edibles like *sukuma wiki* (kale or collard greens), maize, Irish potatoes, sweet potatoes, and tomatoes; in-season fruits such as mangoes from Mombasa and all-seasons fruits like oranges, pawpaws, passion fruits, and bananas of many kinds. Continuing along the way, other stalls contain common Kenyan home necessities such as Omo detergent, hurricane lamps, kerosene lamps, *jiko* (charcoal stoves), "torches" (flashlights), and batteries of various sizes, matches, bags of charcoal, *sufurias* (metal cooking pans), earthen pots of different sizes, silverware, candles, and thermal flasks for hot tea. Used clothes are also abundant at the market, as are *akala* (rubber tire sandals). In sum, most items for sale cater to a population of low income, one that lives without electricity and running water, and with incomes that are both minimal and sporadic.

The Korogocho market is replaced along the road by wattle and daub houses and others made of bricks, all homes densely packed together on both sides of the road. As one reaches the heart of residential Korogocho, garbage and stench aromas pervade the visitor's awareness conditioned by his knowledge that this community experiences frequent outbreaks of cholera. In the middle of Korogocho is a NGO-sponsored feeding center supported by donations where children are fed in hopes of offsetting conditions known to fuel the rapid rise of children entering the streets from this community. Korogocho is a slum where such basic amenities as water are unavailable. Water must be purchased by those who can afford it, often at the expense of food for children. There is a street boy's training center maintained by an expatriate priest who attempts to rehabilitate street boys through training in crafts and artistic productions. These include beautiful *batiks* (dyed cloth) made by the street children that contain scenes of everyday life in the streets.

At the opposite pole of material affluence from Korogocho is the community of Westlands. Street children, whom we studied in Westlands, have developed coping strategies for life in an affluent, socially diverse community. There is a large international-scale economic presence of several large shopping centers, two *Uchumi* (supermarkets), four petrol stations, two busy roundabouts with heavy traffic, banks, one prominent hotel, and many international restaurants (Thai, Chinese, Indian, Italian, etc.). There also is, however, a middle-scale economy in the form of smaller hotels, fast food establishments, bakeries, hair salons, produce shops, car repair and tire shops, bars, and so on. On a still smaller "local" scale, essential items such as fresh food, clothing, fuel, and other necessities are available in a large closed market not visible to the passersby.

Throughout Westlands, similar to the Korogocho market, there are numerous roadside *kiosks* (stalls) where fresh fruits and vegetables abound standing beside stalls with items of used clothing. On a very small scale, Westlands has many roadside corn sellers, candy sellers, shoeshine men, newspaper vendors, and peddlers of bagged fruits, vegetables, and flowers. There are lots of *askaris* (plot guards) in the community, and many employees in the various establishments take buses or *matatus* (small commuter vans or minibuses) to their work in Westlands, often at some distance. Handicapped beggars are strategically scattered around the community, particularly in places where wealthy Kenyans or tourists are likely to be seen (e.g., at a bakery where sweets are sold and the post office). Some of these beggars walk or bus into Westlands on a daily basis. Given its wealthy ambiance, Westlands is one location that attracts street children from communities such as Korogocho as well as from neighboring poor communities.

One such community is Maasai Village, located only minutes away from the high-priced shopping stores in Sarit Center Mall in Westlands. This is a small slum village within the Parklands Estate, a middle-class area in Nairobi close to Parklands Police Station. Maasai Village developed as an informal residence for unemployed and urban poor as well as casual workers in Westlands and elsewhere. The area accommodates over 2,000 people, the majority of whom are Kamba, Kikuyu, and Luyia, in that order. Most of the residents are single mothers as a result of divorce, separation, and desertion or mothers who were never officially married. Others are homeless victims of tribal clashes in the Rift Valley in the 1990s. These clashes involve alleged attacks by indigenous ethnic residents attempting to drive recent residents from what they perceive to be their homeland.

Income levels in Maasai Village are very low mainly because of unemploy-ment and underemployment.   The incomes for the casual employers range between 600 and 700 shillings per month. The majority of people who do work are petty traders dealing in vegetables, bananas, potatoes, dried fish, and the like. Others are hawkers and like some street children sell waste paper and other recyclable materials. Brewing and selling of such illicit and highly intoxicating local alcoholic drinks as *busaa* (local brew) and *chang'aa* (illicit locally distilled liquor) is common. There is no school in the area, meaning high illiteracy levels. Housing structures are mainly "all plastic" or "all carton," with poor ventilation. Drainage is very poor; therefore footpaths teem with feces and uncollected refuse and waste matter from the households. The only piped water comes from a water point owned privately by an individual living in the nearly middle-class area of Parklands. His water is sold to the residents at 2 shillings (about 5 cents) for a 20-liter jerry can (portable liquid container), for which lines can be seen waiting to buy this basic necessity of life. Pit latrines, which are filthy and usually filled to capacity, are communally used. There are few clinics or dispensaries in the area, forcing residents to travel to the Nairobi City Council–owned clinics at the city center for medical attention. The most common medical problems in the area include dysentery, pneumonia, malaria, malnutrition, and sexually transmitted diseases, all associated in Kenya with poverty.

Many street children who come daily to Westlands live in Kangemi. Kangemi is one of Nairobi's sublocations, situated approximately 8 km west of Nairobi City Center and along the main Nairobi–Nakuru Road. The area itself is divided into three types of settlement: the township, satellite, and farmland. The township and its satellite consist mainly of small, individually owned plots. Most plot owners have put up rental structures.

Kibagare Village in Kangemi is the home of some street children in our study. It is adjacent to Loresho Estate. The latter is a high-class residential estate within the outskirts of Nairobi City. Kibagare Village, in striking contrast, is a slum area with a large population of approximately 10,000 people. Initially, the slum was much larger but was recently razed by the City Council authorities as part of their efforts to curb the mushrooming of slums around high-class and middle-class residential areas, as well as other areas within and around the city. When the Kibagare slum was invaded and demolished by the City Council authorities, many of the residents were forced to leave the area for unknown destinations, at which time some children headed for the streets. Later, many residents returned and reconstructed temporary structures for their own accommodation as well as for renting out. The rental rooms are as cheap as 300–450 Ksh. (Kenya shillings) per month (about $6–$10). In general, the village attracts immigrants from the nearby areas who move around in search of employment opportunities.

Kibagare Village developed as a source of temporary shelter for the poorly paid families, divorcees, the separated and widowed, and those with other social and economic problems. Recent ethnic clashes in the Rift Valley have also forced some of the homeless victims to move to the village. The village elders do the allocation of plots in the slum area on a temporary basis. Women head many, if not the majority, of the households, especially those in which young children are found. Unmarried men also head other households. In Kibagare the average household size is 6.2 persons, quite crowded given the small size of most houses.

The majority of the Kibagare Village residents are unemployed. A few are employed as casual workers in the construction industry and other private enterprises while many others engage in hawking and other informal income-generating activities. The village has very few licensed bars, food kiosks and canteens meaning that illegal business practices are widespread. The women, for example, brew illicit drinks like *chang'aa* and *busaa* as sources of income. Drunkenness is widespread in the area, among both men and women. Theft is also unsurprisingly rampant in the area. Those suspected of or caught stealing are taken to the village elders for screening and possible disciplinary action. Serious cases are either forwarded to the police or settled through "mob justice" ending lynching in some cases.

In Kibagare Village, the majority of housing structures are made of carton and plastic materials. A few have timber walls, concrete floors, and corrugated iron sheet roofs. There is serious overcrowding and poor ventilation. There are only one primary school and one secondary school in the entire area, both at the Good News Kibagare Center under the sponsorship of the Missionary Frontiers. Both schools, St. Martin's Primary and Secondary, provide free education for children from poor families in the village, including some street children rehabilitated by the institutions. Special considerations are given to the children from the neglected and destitute families as well as those with poverty-stricken, unemployed parents. The Good News Kibagare Center runs a clinic/dispensary to provide health services in collaboration with UNICEF. Feeding programs are sponsored by the Missionary Frontiers at the Center, catering currently to over 2,000 children from the village as well as rehabilitated street children.

For most households in Kibagare Village, refuse is scattered around everywhere with only a few households burning their garbage. The City Council provides no refuse collection services to the village. The majority of residents use piped water, but drainage is very poor in the area, and there are no bathrooms. Instead, people use their rooms during the day or bathe outside in the open during the night. For drinking, some people use dirty untreated river water, and a few people use rainwater during the rainy season. For fecal disposal there are a few poorly maintained communal pit latrines, each of which is often shared by as many as 15 households, or about 90 people. Some people use the nearby bush. Defecation by preschool children is found all over, at times being thrown away by the elder children or mothers or more usually left to be eaten by the dogs. The major health problems in the area, like other communities in Nairobi, are cold weather, lack of water and food, crowded conditions and medical problems such as pneumonia, diarrhea, measles, malaria, burns, malnutrition and sexually transmitted diseases.

Adjacent to some slums and elsewhere are self-contained bungalows in the better estates, which are rented or owned by affluent or upwardly mobile. For some homeowners in these estates and in some other estates for all owners who work in organizations, collective rates for land plots or houses are available through cooperative arrangements, such as those provided for workers at the University of Nairobi and various other large public institutions. Private homeowners typically mortgage their homes through a bank at a high rate of interest, usually about 25%. Homes in such estates often contain a small servants' quarters used most frequently for a relative from the rural area who works as a housemaid or as an *ayah* (babysitter). Such workers are often paid little money for working seven days a week in exchange for room and board. Child labor advocates frequently decry such working arrangements, which too often involve children under sixteen years of age. It is estimated that ten thousand new homes are needed in Nairobi each year just to keep pace with the aspirations of those who can afford housing. Indeed, owning a house is a dream that the majority of Kenyans living in Nairobi will not be able to fulfill. A new concept seeking to meet housing demand uses cheaper metal and concrete technology to replace older brick and tile-constructed homes in new settlement schemes located on the outskirts of the city.

NAIROBI: "GREEN CITY IN THE SUN"

The majority (80%) of Kenyans live in rural areas where electricity and running water are often not available, and roads are usually not paved. Rural homes are commonly constructed of wattle and daub and thatch, although the wealthiest people do have access to more elaborate constructed homes of stone or brick and frequently live near towns where electricity and running water are available. As a result of significant rural-to-urban migration since independence in 1963, about 25% of Kenyans currently live in cities such as Nairobi, Mombasa, Kisumu, and Nakuru.

Kenyan cities reproduce national social stratification between the rich and poor as is evident in comparing, for instance, Westlands with Kibagare Village. In every city, often within eyesight of affluent communities, there are shanty neighborhoods in which houses are built out of packing cases, flattened tin cans, cardboard, and the familiar wattle and daub used in rural areas. These shantytowns are breeding grounds for theft, prostitution, and excessive alcohol and other drug use. Street children who come from rural areas and urban shantytowns are seen in large numbers in all Kenyan cities and increasingly in towns as well. Nairobi, however, is by far Kenya's largest city, with extremes of wealth and poverty in what is perhaps the most serious social outcome of this city's rapid and unplanned demographic and urban growth since independence. Indeed, the distribution of Kenya's income is among the most unequal in the world (Holmquist, Weaver, & Ford, 1994).

In this section, we confine ourselves to a specific discussion of Nairobi in relation to street children who live there. Fortunately, we can rely on a comprehensive resource for the urban geography and urbanization of Nairobi that contains an excellent series of articles appearing in a special issue of *African Urban Quarterly* devoted to Nairobi (Obudho, 1992). Much of the following material about Nairobi is summarized from this collection, which draws on data that we consider most relevant to our understanding of the urban ecology of street children. Nairobi began as a center to service the British colonialist's quest for administration, entertainment and health. Obudho and Aduwo (1992) have, for example, shown how in 1910 the city of Nairobi had become the main administrative and residential center for most of the settlers because of its "malaria-free" location and the cool temperatures in its western side.   Eventually, residential arrangements developed to reflect sectional cleavages with the Europeans and Asians being found in the hilly western locations and the Africans confined to the eastern areas that were characterized by waterlogged, black soils.

POPULATION

Nairobi's population is now larger than the 1993 estimate of about 2.5 million people and, with a recently estimated 4% annual growth rate, is one of the highest growth rates in the world. This city has over the years consistently grown at a dramatic rate. Nairobi originated in June 1899 as a railway depot midway between Mombasa on the Indian Ocean and Kisumu on Lake Victoria. The railway, sometimes called the "Lunatic Express" (Miller, 1971), was a key factor in the European settlement of East Africa, for which Nairobi became a significant commercial, administrative, and political center city for European settlers and subsequently became Kenya's national capital after the 1963 independence. For many years, both before and after independence, Nairobi was considered as "the city in the sun" for tourists from abroad. Tourists flocked to Nairobi to enjoy its attraction as a terminus to game parks, Indian Ocean beaches, and rich indigenous cultures such as the Maasai in Kenya and to other attractions in neighboring countries of Uganda and Tanzania.

At independence, Nairobi's population was 266,795. The majority of residents at this time were Africans (155,388), with a significant number of Europeans (21,476) and Asians (87,454) (Obudho & Aduwo, 1992, p. 58). Asians were originally brought to East Africa by the British to work on the railway. Later, Asians were permitted to take up business and commercial activities forbidden to Africans. Europeans and Asians, according to the racist colonial policy, resided in ethnic locations with more favorable schools, hospitals, and overall better housing and services compared to Africans. The head start provided to Europeans and Asians by the colonial system of privilege has persisted into the present. Overall, people of Asian and European origin have been shielded by economic affluence from the consequences of poverty and the rapid and dislocated demographic explosion that has affected the poor segments of the Kenyan community composed of segments of indigenous ethnic groups. Street children, for example, do not include children of Asian or European origin, nor do Asians or Europeans reside in slum areas such as Korogocho, Maasai Village and other feeder areas for street children.

Primarily because of an unforeseen and unplanned-for demographic explosion, Kenya—and Nairobi, specifically—have had severe problems in coping with urbanization, a result of the heavy movement of indigenous Africans from rural areas to Nairobi to escape rural poverty. This migration set in motion Kenyans in search of employment and better educational and medical services than are available in the rural areas. National development has not emphasized rural areas in comparison to Nairobi and other cities, which are places where well-to-do Kenyans of all races prefer to reside. In Nairobi, one can experience all the comforts and lifestyle attractions available in Europe and America. Kenya's rapid rate of population growth is also due in significant part to improving medical facilities, which have reduced infant mortality rates and enhanced longevity.

INCOME VARIATION

While European and Asian Kenyans have largely escaped the effects of poverty endured by millions of Kenyans, there are, nevertheless, thousands of indigenous Africans who are wealthy. In Nairobi, in 1992 for example, 60% of "low" earners earned less than 2,300 Ksh. (about $45) a month compared to the 20% of "high earners" who made over 10,000 Ksh. (about $200) a month. The "high" earners group accounts for about 55% of total income in the city compared to the majority "low" wage earners, who garner less than 24% of Nairobi's monthly wages. Still, the "low" income workers, making up the bulk of such occupations as drivers, secretaries, clerks in the formal sector and the *jua kali* (informal sector), street hawkers, flower sellers, and shoe shiners are far better off than the 30 to 40% of adult urbanites who are unemployed. It is estimated that the low-income group spends 56% of its income on food alone such that "they cannot, therefore, afford to pay very much for housing. In fact, on average, this group spends 14.2% of their income on rent" (Syagga & Kiamba, 1992, p. 79). Although housing is a priority for the urban poor, they have comparatively meager resources at their disposal for their crucial needs, and the unemployed have no resources. In the slum of Pumwani, for example, 38.4% are unemployed, and of the employed about one-third of them are in casual or temporary employment. For the employed, the average income is only 1,060 Ksh. (about $21) per month.

In Pumwani, primarily made up of low income urban poor, 78% of the 14,960 residents are tenants. Ninety-four percent live in homes of only two rooms, with an average of four persons living in a room. As for the construction materials, 80% of the houses are made of mud and wattle walls, which is not as bad as some other slum areas where houses are constructed from paper and other odds and ends. Nevertheless, only thirteen communal toilets serve 97% of the residents. Paul Syagga and J. M. Kiamba (1992) conclude their discussion of Pumwani by observing that the community is "inhabited by the poor and the majority of them live in very poor housing characterized by lack of services, lack of community facilities, overcrowding and generally poor sanitation" (p. 84). Street children come from communities such as Pumwani (and adjacent Majengo), where the social environment is characterized by poor nutritional and educational resources for children. Parents, as we have seen, are hard pressed simply to provide rent and food requirements within the fragile monthly budget of their low income earnings, not to mention the hardships experienced by their unemployed neighbors who, with them, make up the "urban poor."

EDUCATION

Many street children come to the streets from places like Korogocho and Pumwani after being forced by poverty to leave school. We have seen in our focus group discussions and life stories the considerable extent to which street children in our research aspire to return to school and regret coming to the streets after leaving school because of poverty. Many who run away from school are in fact "pushed out" by unfavorable home environments inconsistent with the values and life goals emphasized in school. Dropout rates for primary school are dramatic in Kenya, affecting not only the street children. Kevin Lillis (1992) writes about elementary education in Nairobi, "as elsewhere in Kenya, there are high dropout rates. For example, of the 1979 standard one intake, 64.7% did not reach standard eight in 1986. Between 1985 and 1986, 19.2% of boys and 30.1% of girls dropped out of primary school between standard one and eight" (p. 72). The dropouts are alarmingly high from the urban poor families. According to Lillis, alcohol and drug problems, lack of motivation, involvement in home businesses such as selling charcoal and caring for siblings, are all problems encountered by children who aspire to attend school in poor Nairobi neighborhoods. In 1989, according to Lillis, standard eight schooling required about 1,000 Ksh. for essential textbooks alone. Additional costs such as those for uniforms, food, bus fare, swimming, and stationery costs are requirements beyond the basic fees. Little wonder that the dropout rate is not even higher. Secondary school is but a dream, well beyond the economic means of virtually all urban poor. For example, concerning secondary school, Lillis (1992) writes, "Average per capital income in the city of Nairobi in 1989 was 6,000 Ksh., all of which could be spent on educating one child for one year in public secondary school" (p. 74).

A recent study on school enrollment by gender in Kenya indicates that the enrollment of boys and girls at lower primary level is almost the same ranging from 50–59% for boys and 50–41% for girls (Central Bureau of Statistics, 1998). This study also shows that more girls tend to dropout as they approach upper primary level, especially when they are in standard six and seven. Enrollment rate in Kenyan secondary schools shows even greater gender disparity as boys far outnumber the girls (Ministry of Education, 1999). The Central Bureau of Statistics' study shows the main reasons for school dropout as lack of fees (41.4%), sociocultural prejudices against the girl child and gender stereotypes (20.5%), lack of interest (14.2%), and marriage (8.5%) among others. North-Eastern Province has the highest female dropout rate (72%), primarily because of Islam. Most Muslim parents tend to withdraw their female children from school before they complete primary education, and they are married early.

CLIMATE AND AIR QUALITY

Street children are directly impacted by Nairobi's climate. Nairobi is located near the Equator with a mean altitude of 1,700 meters above sea level. Its climate is influenced primarily by trade winds from the north and southeast. There are two wet seasons; the long rains are centered in April, with a short rainy season centered in November. Some westerly winds and heavy cloud covers are common from June through August when Nairobi because of its altitude can become quite chilly especially at night. The street children are not able to collect waste papers for sale during the rainy season, because buyers will not buy wet products from them. This is very stressful for them, for the long rains can last for two months. During the "cool" season in June, July, and August street children are hard hit by respiratory infections and complain of being cold at night.

Although individual activities in Nairobi are primarily confined to "the industrial area," air pollution from suspended particulate pollutants in the industrial area has reached high concentration levels. Moreover, carbon monoxide, nitrogen oxide, and sulfur oxide emitted by cars, trucks, and buses have been found to be very high during rush hours, in particular near roundabouts, where street children are frequently concentrated. This has contributed to their consistent respiratory problems and long-term health hazards as well. Francis Situma (1992) reports, "Kenya uses leaded gasoline for all its vehicles. About 20% of the fuel released by an automobile engine is released as poison into the air" (p. 172).

GARBAGE

The "green city in the sun" designation is now but a distant memory in the minds of older Nairobi residents. Instead, the term "garbage city" (Odegi-Awuondo, Haggai, & Mutsotso, 1994, p. 46) appropriately symbolizes current images of slums, of citywide garbage, squalor, and potted roads resembling in places a battlefield, and of street children. "Currently, the degree and efficiency of solid waste collection and disposal in the city of Nairobi is inadequate with unsightly heaps of refuse rotting in people's backyards and shopping centers" (Otieno, 1992, p. 142). Plastic, tin, paper, vegetable, and other social waste products provide breeding grounds for flies, mosquitoes, and rodents contributing to the health hazards of street children who scavenge through dustbins for food and frequently sleep at night near refuse areas. In Nairobi, burning and dumping are common means of disposal, with not infrequent dumping along the streets and between houses. Garbage collection by Nairobi City Council is sporadic and frequently unpredictable even in affluent residential areas. On this point, Situma (1992) writes, "In the slum areas refuse collection is never done. The same is true of high-income areas such as

Upperhill, Milimani, Parklands and Westlands. The result is that small children, goats and dogs scavenge on the garbage" (p. 169).

Street children, as we will see later, are involved in a significant way in the removal and recycling of garbage. Casper Odegi-Awuondo, Haggai W. Namai and Beneah M. Mutsotso (1994) have studied the garbage collection of Nairobi. They write in *Masters of Survival* that, "There is a connection between the toilet roll, exercise books, wrapping paper, paper bags into which sugar is carried, envelops, etc. in the groceries and the dirty, ill clad and strange looking garbage collectors in the streets of the city. The rubbish scavenged from the dustbin is what is recycled to produce those items listed above" (p. 45). In their survey of 256 garbage collectors, Odegi-Awuondo et al. found that 95% were over-whelmingly young males, two-thirds being between 13 and 35 years of age. About one-half were married. Although most of his garbage collectors lived in the slums, often with families, Odegi-Awuondo et al. (1994) were told that quite a number of them "sleep in the streets in the open and we think are, therefore, street children" (p. 57). Their findings are in agreement with some of our own observations. For example, two-thirds of the garbage collectors gave paper as their top collected item, one that is available only in the dry season as buyers purchase only dry paper for recycling. Collectors 'go hungry' for days in the wet season. He calculated that his 1989 data showed a 73 shillings a day average income with a minimum daily income of a meager 5 shillings and a maximum of about 622 shillings a day.

MIGRATION

Although Nairobi's natural increase has been high, rural to urban migration has been the most significant social dynamic in Kenya since independence. Nairobi has had an extraordinarily high annual fertility growth rate of 4.7% per year between 1979 and 1989 (Obudho & Aduwo, 1992, p. 58). The two notable demographic factors in the migration to Nairobi are that the city's population is overrepresented by males (58% male in 1979), and it is young. For 1979, less than 3% of the population was over 60 and about 30% of males and 43% of females were 14 and under (all demographic figures after Obudho & Aduwo, 1992).

The social organization of the city reflects its overall migratory and youthful population. Consequently street children live "distorted" lifestyles but within broad normative urban social patterns that are themselves in turn distortions of indigenous, rural norms of social organization. Aylward Shorter has written an informative book entitled, *The Church in the African City* (1991), that contains important sociological insights about Nairobi's emergent forms of social organization. Shorter states that a 1986 Nairobi City survey revealed "a majority of the population paid at least five visits a year to the rural areas. . . . They tend to return to the homeland in order to marry, give birth, or retire. Usually they maintain a rural family home as well as an urban residence" (p.

15). The idea that Nairobi is where one has a "house" (for work) in contrast to the rural area that is the "home," where one is buried, is significant for understanding most Nairobi residents today. Shorter (1991) reports further that parishioners routinely maintain affiliations in both a Nairobi and a rural parish. The anonymity of the city permits many young migrants "freedom" from community and family sanctions controlling their behavior at home. Sexual relations, clothing styles, expenditures, and the like take on an urban "bright lights" atmosphere, one in which street children also seek to participate.

Urban households frequently are of the "bachelor" sort, with unmarried men and women sharing social networks while working, *tar macking* (looking for jobs), and seeking job training and other educational opportunities. Numerous female-headed family households and the absence of extended families in Nairobi offer additional contrasts to rural values. Slum areas depart further still from these values to the extent that poverty dictates a breakdown of any organized family life at all. In its place is a constant preoccupation with finding money for rent or food. An excellent novel, *Going Down River Road*, by Meja Mwangi (1976), describes how life in a Nairobi shantytown is fraught with the most brittle form of family and gender relations imaginable, lived out in the midst of constant migration from place to place in search of material security and friendship. Not infrequently, for example, one's house is literally torn down by city authorities in front of one's eyes merely because one is a squatter and therefore has no legal residential rights.

Shorter (1991) reports a growth of religious indifference in Nairobi compared to rural areas. He cites data that show that 73% of the nation's population is Christian, with 40% of these attending church weekly in rural areas compared to only 12% attending in Nairobi where "60% never go near a church" (p. 74). Speaking about the Nairobi young (presumably including some street children about whom he writes elsewhere in his book), Shorter (1991) states that "sport, music, dancing, film shows and bars draw them to the urban areas. Bars and discos bear names that echo the leisure ethic . . . Delight, . . . Comfort, . . . Shade, . . . Love-Boat Inn, Broadway, Cloud Nine, etc. (p. 116). Nevertheless, Shorter points out that in this world of glorified "stadium, stage and screen" most young people want to work. We also found this to be true of street children in our study as described in our material on focus group interviews. In fact, the rest of the story about the generally depressing urban slums is that they constitute what Shorter refers to as "a self-help city." Frequent self-initiative and entrepreneurial activities serve as a source of optimism and a symbol of aspirations for the urban poor. Shorter (1991) optimistically writes, perhaps with numerical exaggeration, "a visit to a shanty town reveals that every other dwelling houses a business of one kind or another: vegetable stalls, food kiosks, shoecraft, tailoring, shoe shining, carpentry, stone masonry, tin smithing, radio repair, car washing, photography" (p. 55).

STREET CHILDREN AND MIGRATION

The street children and their families who participated in our survey basically conform to the social patterns described above for Nairobi's general population. First they represent, on the whole, a significant migratory experience for both children and their families. Fifty-three percent of the surveyed street children were born in the slums of Nairobi. The rest were born in Central (26%), Eastern (9%), Western (6%), Nyanza (4%), and North-Eastern Provinces (2%). Most of these children born in the rural areas later came to Nairobi either alone or in the company of friends or relatives to seek ways to support themselves. Some of the children in our sample were victims of tribal clashes who had been misplaced from their homes in parts of Rift Valley, Western, and Nyanza Provinces. A number of these children and their families found their way to Nairobi and eventually ended up on the streets.

Ethnic comparisons indicated that 66% of the parents were Kikuyu, historically the dominant ethnic group in the vicinity. The others were Luo (14.3%), Abaluyia (10.7%), Kamba (7.4%) and Meru (2.1%). Overall, most of the parents were migrants who originally came from different parts of the country, including rural areas near Nairobi. As shown in Table 4.1, nearly 60% of the parents originally came from Central Province, out of which 28% came from Murang'a district within 50 miles of Nairobi. Currently, the parents in our study were staying in the various slums in Nairobi such as Mathare, Korogocho, Kibera, Kawangware, Majengo, and Kangemi, among others.

Inadequate access to land, coupled with limited rural employment opportunities, have greatly contributed to rural to urban migration. The landless, whose plots have been fragmented into small, unviable units, have tended to move to Nairobi and other urban centers to look for ways of making a living. Only 22.4% of the parents in the sample had some land. The remaining 77.6% said they were landless. About 77% of the parents said they had lived in Nairobi for over ten years. Most of them had no plans to move to another place in the future. The main reasons for coming to Nairobi were given as employment (53.1%) and marriage (39.8%).

Landlessness among women is also attributed to barriers with regard to land inheritance. This is a structural constraint, borne out of a patriarchal authority system in which women lack access to property inheritance. The size of land holdings for poor households has diminished as a result of high population growth rate and privatization and fragmentation of land. It should, however, be noted that there is enough quality land for those who have money to pay for it. Of those parents who had land, 45.5% had only 1–3 acres of land, 18.2% had 3–5 acres, and a further 22.7% owned over 5 acres. Only 13.6% had less than an acre of land. The majority of the parents were not only landless, but they had no other property as well. Those who said they had no property of their own accounted for 92.9% of the sample. The few who had some property said that their property was in Nairobi (85.7%), as compared to a mere 14.3% who had some property in the rural areas.

Table 4.1
Original Home of Parents

Original Home	N	%
Murang'a	28	28.6
Nyeri	14	14.3
Kiambu	10	10.2
Siaya	8	8.1
Kakamega	6	6.1
Makueni	4	4.1
Machakos	3	3.1
Nyandarua	3	3.1
Kirinyaga	3	3.1
Nairaobi	3	3.1
Bungoma	3	3.1
Kangundo	3	3.1
Homa Bay	2	2.0
Vihiga	2	2.0
Kitui	2	2.0
Meru	2	2.0
Kisumu	1	1.0
Wajir	1	1.0
Total	98	100.0

SOCIOECONOMIC BACKGROUND OF FAMILIES OF STREET CHILDREN

Social, economic, and demographic characteristics of the families in our survey conform to the patterns described for the urban poor in Nairobi. Our sample of 98 parents included 16 males and 82 females who ranged in age from 28 to 60 with an average age of 37 years. Most of the parents (71.4%) were aged between 31 and 40 years, and 18.4% were over 40. Table 4.2 shows the age distribution of the parents. The parents are, on the whole, young with about 80% under 40 years of age.

With regard to marital status, there were more unmarried parents in the sample than those who said they had spouses. Those who were not married accounted for 62.1% of our sample. Out of the total sample, 67.0% were heads of households. Another 18.6% of the parents reported that their fathers were household heads. These were single mothers who were staying with their parents while their own children were on the streets. For the female household heads, the women were heading their own households either because they had never been married before (12.2%), they were divorced (23.4%), their husbands had died (26.5%), or they had separated from abusive and neglectful men who had abandoned them and married other women (21.4%). No doubt, these results indicate that most of the street children in our sample were from female-headed households. Rapid population growth has frequently been cited as one of the factors associated with the existence of street children. With regard to siblings, about 39% of the parents had between 2 and 3 living children. Another 55% had 4 to 7, and 6.2% had over 7 children. The average parent had 4 children. Thus, most of the surveyed children come from large and impoverished urban families.

On educational levels, approximately 62% of the parents had 1 to 4 years of primary education, and another 17% had between 5 to 8 years. The remaining 21.3% had no formal education. The average parent had left school in lower primary and was semi-literate. Occupations of families in our survey also reflect a low educational level. About 56% of the parents, for example, were petty commodity traders with very low and irregular incomes; 9.7% were beggars on the streets; 11.8% of the mothers said they were housewives; 6.5% were in formal employment; 6.5% were brewing *busaa* and selling *chang'aa* in the slums, and 5.4% were barmaids. Except for a distinct minority, the bulk of the surveyed parents (81.9%) were desperately poor, with deadend occupations because they lacked marketable skills. Many of the female parents, including the barmaids, often supplemented their low incomes from hawking and vending various commodities, including commercial sex.

Table 4.2
Age Distribution of Parents

Age	N	%
28 to 30	10	10.2
31 to 35	36	36.7
36 to 40	34	34.7
41 to 49	14	14.3
50 to 60	4	4.1
Total	98	100.0

Table 4.3
Monthly Income of Parents

Monthly Income (Kenya Shillings)	N	%
500	11	11.1
500 to 1,000	65	66.3
1,000 to 1,500	7	7.1
1,500 to 2,000	2	2.1
No response	13	13.3
Total	98	100.0

The majority of the surveyed parents were involved in a wide range of low-paying jobs in the informal sector. The average monthly income was 775 shillings. Their monthly incomes ranged from 300 to 2000 shillings with 63.6% of them earning between 500 to 1000 shillings; most of the parents were thus living below the subsistence level without enough money to meet their families' basic needs. Most of these parents were unable to care for their children. Over 69% of the parents had more than one child in the streets. Most of them were male children. The average number of street children from each family was two, and in some cases the whole family was on the streets, either working or living there or both. Parents said the main reason children were on the streets was to look for money for themselves (76.2%) and their families (13.9%).

Chapter 5

Kenyan Voices: Focus Group and Survey Responses

I squeezed into an already crowded "matatu" with six street children who had agreed to accompany me to the university where Enos Njeru had engaged a room so as to enable us to collect focus group materials from the street boys. Earlier we had obtained such materials from both a male and a female group of University of Nairobi adult employees. Still later, the next year, street girls responded to the same questions asked of the other three groups for comparisons to consider potential gender attitudes. After reaching the university, Enos Njeru welcomed the boys, who had positioned themselves around the small lecture room. Midway in the exercise, led by Enos Njeru in Kiswahili, one of the street boys left abruptly, as we later learned, to get glue. He had been silent for some time after eagerly participating in the group discussions. Abruptly, the boy, a key informant of mine, asked to be excused and headed for the door. Several days later he was given the last (of three) questions which he had missed, all three having been given in turn to the various groups mentioned above for their focused discussion. The following summer further methodological flexibility was required with street girls who were participating in our focus group discussions (as with the boys in Kiswahili, but this time led by a research assistant). At the outset a street boy, very high on glue, stood in the background mumbling the questions over and over while asking for money. He occasionally seemed to me to disrupt the "flow" of group discourse; in fact, he seemed of little concern to the girls if not to me. (Kilbride field notes, 1995, 1996)

In the summer of 1994, P. K. and E. N. organized two focus group sessions on the topic of street children, one with men, the other with women. All participants were employed by the University of Nairobi in the capacity of support staff and were known by the authors. The women numbered eight and were employed as secretaries, with the exception of one woman who was a lecturer. The men numbered five, all of whom worked as clerks or middle level administrators.   With the exception of the female lecturer, none of the participants had university education, but all had secondary school and some form of professional school training. The participants came from a variety of ethnic groups (Kikuyu, Luo, Abaluyia, Kamba) and were, therefore, representative of ethnic variation in the nation. Adult groups such as ours, made up as they were of participants with similar educational backgrounds, are thought to be ideally suited for maximum participation in discussion (Merton, Fiske, & Kendall, 1990). Indeed, there was a slight tendency for the university-educated person in the adult woman's group to be more verbal and articulate than the others. She, however, did not dominate discussion to the point of raising concern about a "leader effect" (Merton, Fiske & Kendall, 1990) nor could any participants be said to show a reluctance to speak often or thoroughly. We had hoped to get between 5 and 10 participants for each group following the reasoning of Merton et al. (1990), who advise that a focus group "should not be so large as to be unwieldy or to preclude adequate participation by most members nor should it be so small that it fails to provide substantially greater coverage than that of an interview with one individual" (p. 137). While all participants were favorable about our project, we nevertheless provided a small renumeration at the end of the several hours graciously given to us by Kenyans concerned about the plight of street children in their country.

In 1995 we invited six street boys to the campus of the University of Nairobi to participate in a focus group discussion. The boys ranged in age from 13 to 17 years. Their time on the streets varied from two to ten years. Three boys were Kikuyu; the other three were Luyia, Kamba, and Coastal Swahili. None of the boys' education exceeded primary school, although all boys had some formal education. In 1996, we organized a focus group session with some street girls. The street girls were not as well-known to us as were the boys, with whom we had been involved for several years. We relied on the help of one girl whom we knew well to help us get volunteers. As with the boys, we offered the girls a small payment for cooperation. The children needed money, and the idea of working for payment was reasonable to them and consistent with our desire to employ the children as our assistants whenever possible. Our informant located five other girls, so that our focus groups numbered six. All of these girls were Kikuyu. All had some schooling and had been on the streets for at least one year. Four girls were extremely verbal. One apparently shy girl did contribute, unlike another quiet girl who seemed mentally slow. Overall, our street children focus groups seemed to represent the range of variation we had observed more generally among street girls and boys.

Requiring some flexibility as indicated in the ethnographic vignette, it took a great deal of time to get all the participants in the same place at the same time, but with adaptability and patience, we found the focus group technique to be useful and feasible. This technique was well within the social tendencies of street children to be on the whole "verbal" and conversational, especially with questions concerning their own experiences with life on the streets. We found that street children, by drawing on their own experiences, frequently had stories of their own to be told concerning solutions for the street children problem, the subject of one of our questions. The adults too were eager participants. Indigenous cultural practices emphasize storytelling as a cherished educational and recreational tradition (Taban lo Liyong, 1972). At the same time, personality preferences in Kenya favor a gregarious, "talkative" style over "silence" or "rugged individualism" (Kilbride & Kilbride, 1990).

Three focus group discussions were held in a lecture room with Kilbride and Njeru asking questions in a conversational format so as to encourage the informality desired in focus group techniques. The adults were questioned in English, the boys in Kiswahili. Njeru was the focus group leader for all sessions held at the university. For the adults, seating arrangements were around a table in a conference room with the investigators seated among focus group participants. P. K. passed the tape recorder around while E. N. kept conversation going. The street boys were spread out in a lecture hall, although the investigators sat among them, once again to encourage informality, a key objective in the focus group technique (Merton, Fiske & Kendall, 1990).

The street girls were questioned in a quiet, shaded, outdoor corner of the university used by staff for resting during breaks; however, we chose a time when only our group was present. Our research assistant, a man in his early twenties, led the discussion in Kiswahili. He was already well-known to some of the girls, whom he had previously interviewed. Informality was encouraged not only by the setting and familiar interviewers but also by the presence of a few familiar onlookers, including the street boy mentioned above. The girls, like the boys, enjoyed hearing their voices on the tape recorder after the sessions were completed.

Adults and children were asked three questions: "What is a street child?" "Why are there street children in Kenya?" and "What should be done about street children?" (e.g., to help them, to eliminate them). Questions were asked of each participant in turn, and when discussion had ended on a question, the procedure was repeated for the next question until all of the questions were thoroughly discussed. These questions were open ended and were selected after consideration of how best to elicit the opinions of local Kenyans concerning the problem of street children and suggestions for possible solutions, taking into account what street children themselves think about this. By reporting here the voices of street children, we are able to address policy issues in chapter 10.

RESULTS

Tables 5.1 and 5.2 present in reductive form the range of responses to the question "What is a street child?" The children's responses were easily more expansive (10 traits compared to 3) than those of their adult counterparts.

Adults tended to make more generalized groups while the children provided more concrete examples of behaviors and characteristics. Their firsthand knowledge of street life and a firsthand focus on their present situation of perceived deprivation may have contributed to what may be a difference of cognitive saliency. Significantly, however, both adults and children agree that family poverty, as a general diagnostic condition, is a key diagnostic trait, one that in turn affects the child's family situation and especially its inability to provide food. It is very important also to note here that adults and children both do not isolate the child, in this case the street child, from his/her family context. This perception is a very important family cultural value in Kenya.   More specifically, all respondents think first and foremost that a street child is one necessarily in search of food, especially in dirty places. This finding recalls our earlier discussion of the semantic meaning of the Swahili word *chokora* (street child). What is surprising is the relative extent to which food deprivation rather than sleeping away from home is emphasized by both adults and children. Perhaps the most interesting difference for policy implications (see chapter 10) is that two of the children emphasized "working" (as paper collectors) while none of the thirteen adults indicated any verbalized awareness that street children are, in fact, frequently children who work to get money.

Tables 5.3 and 5.4 present the results of our second question, "Why are there street children in Kenya?" All four groups agreed that "poverty" was a key reason while for the adult's "family breakdown," especially divorce, was also important. The children, too, considered family problems very significant but were more precise about specific parental concerns that they had experienced or heard about from others. In addition to poverty, the children mentioned such familial problems as parental beatings, abandonment, alcoholism, and lack of love as causal factors. Only the boys were concerned about prostitutes and mothers often abandoning their children, whereas only the girls discussed beatings by parents, with one mentioning being beaten at an approved school. Both adult women and street boys raised family-related problems such as adolescent pregnancies, single motherhood, a high birth rate, and a lack of "family planning." Parents sending children out to the streets to beg is another issue that was discussed by adult women and street boys. Only the street boys raised the problem of persistent, annual inflated food cost, a concern that reflects their own work situation as they try to make a subsistence living as collectors of paper and other waste products. Street children's insider view of street life highlighted the role that street children themselves play in recruiting other children to the streets. One girl emphasized that street life is very addictive and, therefore, difficult to break away from even if given chances to do so. The adult women in our focus group considered street children reproducing families to be a significant factor in the rise of street children numbers in recent years. One woman felt that more government programs were needed to curb this dramatic rise. Rural to urban migration is, these adults strongly believe, at the heart of many urban social problems, especially as far as street children are concerned.

Table 5.1
What is a Street Child? (Adults)

Responses	Women	Men	Both
Poor child looking for food	6	3	9
Child running away from home problems (divorce, abuse)	2	1	3
Discarded illegitimate children (some born on the streets)	1	3	4

Table 5.2
What is a Street Child? (Street Boys and Girls)

Responses	Boys	Girls	Both
Eats from dust bin (waste food, spoiled, rotten food, garbage)	4	1	5
From poor family	4	1	5
Glue addiction	2	2	4
One who does not shower, always dirty	1	2	3
Sleeps out (anywhere), disturbed by street boys at night while sleeping out	2	1	3
Begging only but lives at home, always begs	1	1	2
Paper collection	2	0	2
Dresses badly	2	0	2
Does not go home	1	0	1
Domestic problems (violence, quarrelling, dead parents)	1	0	1

Table 5.3
Why are there Street Children in Kenya? (Adults)

Responses	Women	Men	Both
Poverty (lack of jobs due to education)	4	5	9
Family breakdown (divorce)	3	5	8
Adolescent pregnancy	2		2
Single motherhood	2		2
Street children reproducing	2		2
Rural-urban migration	4	2	6
Begging encouraged by parents, and necessity for begging	2		2
Refugee problems and ethnic clashes		2	2
Lack of family planning	1		1
Not enough governmental programs	1		1

Table 5.4
Why are there Street Children in Kenya? (Street Boys and Girls)

Responses	Boys	Girls	Both
Poor people, family poverty, unemployed parents	6	3	9
Street children recruiting others	2	2	4
Beaten by parents, beaten by drunken mother, beaten at approved school		4	4
Inflation of food costs	3		3
Prostitutes abandoning their children	3		3
Insufficient food, clothing and parental love at home	1		1
Alcoholic parents	1		1
Addiction to street life		1	1
Unplanned adolescent pregnancies	1		1
High birth rate	1		1
Parents sending children so as to be given money	1		1

Table 5.5
What Should Be Done about Street Children? (Adults)

Responses	Women	Men	Both
Foreign and government aid, foundation grants for rehabilitation	4	1	5
Provide training opportunities or schooling	4	3	7
Collect children from streets and place them with responsible adults or in group homes	3		3
Employ social workers to care for children and teach them proper living skills	2		2
Kenyan men should be more responsible and self-controlled	2		2
Kenyan women should become more self-reliant and self-supporting	1		1
Educate people about family planning	1		1
Educate people about plight of street children	1		1
Form a committee to seek solutions	1		1
Rural development		2	2
Put street children on rural farms for pay	4	4	8

Tables 5.5 and 5.6 describe responses to the question, "What should be done about street children?" The adults and street boys believe, as a matter of high priority, that assistance from personal sponsors, government, and foundations should be increased so as to provide for schooling needs or for technical training in employable skills such as carpentry, tailoring, and so on. Barriers to employment such as the need for "identity cards," the boys believe, should be

eliminated. The boys also think that self-employment should be encouraged and older boys should be hired as a matter of priority. The boys, in keeping with a fundamental characteristic of their social organization, believe that "big" boys should be given jobs and technical training whereas "little" boys should be sent back to school, usually primary school. On the whole, Table 5.6 clearly shows how salient for the boys, especially big ones, is the desire for employment, along with education, as a perceived remedy for street life. While emphasizing education, the adults did not dwell, as did the boys, on employment. This may be due to the fact that the Kenyan public does not have a widespread understanding of the street child as a working child. At the same time, child labor, which is illegal in Kenya, is not a reasonable solution to advocate. Nevertheless, if the public had an accurate image of the child as a willing worker, there would be less need for one boy to advocate that street children be treated with more dignity or as he put it "to be taken as a person."

Table 5.6
What Should Be Done about Street Children? (Street Boys and Girls)

Responses	Boys	Girls	Both
Small boys sent to school	5		5
Older boys sent for training (mechanics, carpentry, polytechnic, tailoring)	3	1	4
Provide food, clothing, and shelter	1	2	3
Older boys given jobs	1	1	2
Get identity cards so as to get employment	2		2
Stop parental beating, alcoholic parental beating		2	2
Respected as a person	1		1
Older boys sent to homes for basic needs	1		1
Grown-up supervision	1		1
Self-employment	1		1
Girls sent to a home to learn domestic chores	1		1
Stop police interference		1	1
Provide family planning		1	1

In general, the answers are, for the adults, abstract and analytical, with an emphasis on institutional, global, and national solutions. Foreign aid, education programs, formation of committees, and rural development all seem reasonable to the adults but are far removed from the immediate daily concerns and needs experienced by the children. The adults, too, were supportive of efforts to forcibly remove children from the streets and to place them in group homes or rural farms to foster opportunities for work, schooling, and rehabilitation. Such programs of forced movement have been attempted already in Kenya without success. Only the women mentioned "moral" issues, urging that social workers should be hired to teach the children how to live properly (avoid sex, protected sexual contact, better hygiene, etc). Two women felt strongly that men should learn to better control their urges to have "outside" children and to visit prostitutes, concentrating instead on better care for the illegitimate children they already have as a result of such activities. It was hoped that these "moral" changes would reduce the pool of children from which street children come.

In our focus group discussion, the street girls were very focused on their most paramount present needs of food, clothing, shelter, family planning services, and protection from the police. Once again they agreed that parental beating was a problem that, if eliminated, would certainly be a positive step in reducing the movement of girls to the streets. Neither returning to school nor obtaining employment, with one exception, were important concerns for the girls. We turn now to a discussion of gender differences.

GENDER

The girls with whom we worked in the summer of 1996 were exclusively girls "of the streets." The girls in our focus group slept out at night and were all separated from their families as compared to the boys, who, although they also slept on the streets, had family ties that were more in evidence to us through visiting and in their communication. The boys were more in agreement with the adults in expressing their overall preference for "school" and "employment" as desired objectives, ones in conformity with national values and goals for Kenyans. By their dependence on survival sex, street girls are further removed from the "mainstream" Kenyan value system than are the boys. On the whole, girls in Kenya have not been encouraged as much as boys to seek formal education so that it is not surprising that most gender comparisons would find boys favoring education more than do girls. To better explore differences between boys and girls, we asked the street children in our focus group a fourth question, "What is the difference between street boys and street girls?"

The girls mentioned a difference in access to work based on gender. One girl said, "A boy takes his *gunia* (bag) and goes in front of the shops so that he is given used and waste papers and cartons to sell and get some money while a street girl can stay the whole day without even getting something to eat. It therefore means that we street girls are suffering a lot because unless someone has sympathized with you by giving you some little money, we can't go and collect the papers the way boys do."

The girls also agreed that they are especially cooperative as compared to boys. One girl reported, for instance, that, "We are so many street girls nowadays in this town and we love each other. If we get something good we divide it among ourselves so that each and everyone gets a share of it. When one has a problem, we help him/her. For example, when one is sick, we take him/her to the hospital so that he is treated." Another girl added her own observations while agreeing with the theme of cooperation, "The difference between me and a street boy is only that I am a girl and the other person is a boy. The boys always do things on their own while the girls like to sit together and do their own things. The boys like to abuse the girls and whenever they see girls sitting together, they come and disorganize us." As this quote and the following suggest, there is a widespread perception by both boys and girls that the boys tend to "beat" the girls and that the girls are at the bottom of the gendered status hierarchy. One girl received strong consent from her cohorts when she said in response to our question about gender differences, "These boys once they have 'taken their things,' i.e. *bhangi* [marijuana], one just comes to where you are and sends you to go buy for him something in the shops and if you refuse to go, he beats you up like a child."

Nevertheless, in spite of perceived gender differences in behavior and social power, the girls in the end think of themselves as one with the boys as a single social category. One girl agreed with another girl who said that the street boys were her "brothers" who do so much together. She added that the term *chokora* applies to both boys and girls because, "We are also *chokora* because we sniff glue, we smoke *bhangi,* and we drink alcohol even in front of our parents and the public in general. You see in that case we can't miss being called *chokora.* Sometimes somebody was eating chips then suddenly that chip falls down and we start fighting over it and as it is picked from the ground or dust then we start eating it."

One girl perceptively described what it feels like to endure the status of *chokora,* a testimony from the bottom of the social hierarchy, which reveals much suffering. She said that a *chokora* is "a dirty person." Your clothes are dirty. Your legs are dirty because you don't have money to buy soap. You don't comb your hair. You look like a mad person, and you even don't have shoes. Sometimes you get water, but you don't want to bathe. You become dirty until people now start to sympathize with you. That is why we are called *chokora* because we become so careless with our own body until we are smelling so that sometimes people don't want to be close to us."

When street girls who are "on" the street are compared to street girls "of" the street, some key differences are evident. We had another focus group encounter with six girls who frequent the Laini Saba market in Kibera, all of whom beg or search for food on a daily basis but sleep home at night (Njeru, Kariuki, & Kilbride, 1995). Some offered points about themselves, which are significant for comparison with the girls "of" the street. All of the girls live with their mothers or grandmothers and take food or money home if they can. Money is needed at home to buy food, paraffin, salt, and other consumer items. Although these girls "on" the street would welcome gifts of clothes, food, and shelter, they emphatically, and in contrast to the girls "of" the street, wanted to go to school. In fact, schooling is, in their opinion, the most important thing that can be done for them. One girl said to the approval of the others, "I would really like to go back to school and learn like other children." Another girl added, "School is most important because I can help my family and myself in future." Like the boys, these street girls eat from garbage heaps and are called *chokora*. To them, food is more of a problem than where to sleep. As one girl said, "You cannot sleep if you eat nothing."

Our focus group work with street girls shows that girls "on the street," like boys both "on" and "of" the street, have ties with home, especially with their mothers and their grandmothers. Such girls, like boys, also value education, regarding highly an opportunity to return to school. In contrast, girls "of the street" are, on the whole, a distinct category that is extremely marginalized from the wider society as compared to their fellow street children.

The Views of Our Surveyed Children on Assistance Priorities

In our survey the street children were asked to indicate which programs they would prefer which would improve their overall situation. Table 5.7 shows their preferred programs.

Table 5.7
Programs Preferred by Street Children

Preferred Programs	N	%
Feeding	100	25.0
Free education	88	22.1
Provision of clothing	79	19.8
Shelter	50	12.5
Training	42	10.4
Employment	20	5.0
Credit scheme	4	1.0
Counseling	3	0.6
No response	14	3.6
Total	400	100.0

The most preferred forms of assistance were feeding, free education, provision of clothing, shelter, and training. Most of the children were not specific on the types of training they needed. This was primarily because of their low levels of education and general lack of awareness of available training options. Those who mentioned training were not able to specify the types of training they would need. The views on vocational training for street children, however, were much better articulated by the NGOs interviewed.

Nearly 83% of the surveyed children reported that they had never participated in any program aimed at improving their situation. The few who said that they had been involved in such programs mostly mentioned feeding at the rescue centers that have been set up by the Undugu (brotherhood) Society in various parts of Nairobi. In the absence of any realistic programs to address their problems, the street children could perhaps see the need to have a welfare association that could cater to their needs. Our study shows that 94% of the surveyed children were not involved in such welfare organizations but offered assistance to their friends as the need arose. Quite a good number of the children in our sample (41%) maintained contact with their families on a regular basis. Another 25% went home occasionally to seek help from parents and other relatives. Nearly 35% said they never returned home for assistance, some of whom were orphans.

PARENTS' VIEWS ABOUT ASSISTANCE FOR THEIR CHILDREN

In our survey when the parents of street children were asked what they thought should be done to keep the children off the streets, 37.8% of them suggested that there should be a policy instrument that guarantees free and compulsory basic education to forestall school dropouts (see Table 5.8). This, they believe, can be achieved through state intervention and sustained by a strong political will. Other parents (21.4%) felt that their impoverished conditions have to be changed before their children can leave the streets and rejoin them at home. They needed to get into some form of employment or income-generating activities. The key issue here is empowerment of the family in order to enhance its caregiving capability. We will address the significance for policy of formal education and family empowerment in chapter 10.

Table 5.8
Parents' Views on What Should Be Done to Keep Children off the Streets

What Should Be Done	N	%
Provide free and compulsory education	37	37.8
Create employment for parents	21	21.4
Provide food to poor families	21	21.4
Help children get into *jua kali* business	4	4.1
Provide credit facilities to parents	3	3.1
Take them to children's home	1	1.0
Don't know	11	11.2
Total	98	100.0

Table 5.9
Parental Plans to Get Children off the Streets

Plans to Withdraw Children from the Streets	N	%
Start/expand income-generating activities	19	19.3
Take the children to the rural areas	16	16.0
Get better paying jobs	11	12.6
Take them to school	11	10.9
Take them to their fathers	7	6.7
Provide vocational training	6	5.9
Buy land and build a house	3	3.4
Provide them with enough food	7	6.7
No plans	18	18.5
Total	98	100.0

Based on the recognition that the problem of street children is too complex to be explained by a single factor and too monumental to be left for one agency, the parents acknowledged that they do have a role to play in keeping their children off the streets. Parents gave their own priority needs as housing (19.3%), children's education (19.3%), employment (18.6%), food (17.4%), land (15.6%), and loan to start business enterprises (9.8%). Many of them had some plans of how to get their children off the streets and to restore their dignity (see Table 5.9).

Strategies of getting the children off the streets, according to the parents, included efforts to start or expand income-generating activities, take the children to the rural areas, get better-paying jobs, look for schools for the children, take them to their fathers, and/or take them for vocational training. Nearly 19% of the parents had no plans to get their children off the streets, at least not in the foreseeable future. They simply had no idea what to do about their own situation and that of their children. Their prospects for a brighter future are dimmed by the sluggish economic growth, dwindling employment opportunities and collapsing families. When the family breaks down, society breaks down.

Chapter 6

Work Patterns, Occupational Spaces, and Survival Strategies

A young street boy, whom we will call Thomas, walked along Westlands Lane early in the morning carrying on his back an empty sack, one that he hoped would, by late afternoon, be filled with waste paper products otherwise known as "karatasi." Such garbage items as, for example, empty milk packets, paper bags, old newspapers, and tin cans were all resources to be sold to entrepreneurs for sale to recycling companies. This boy, 15 years old, wore only one old shoe, a pair of long trousers and a short-sleeved shirt, each with tears sufficient for me to recall the term "tattered" as he walked along the road. After greeting me, Thomas continued along in the opposite direction down the badly potholed, dust-stained tarmac lane heading out of Westlands towards the "Casino" about a mile away and a good place to find karatasi. Westlands Lane runs parallel to Waiyaki Way, a busy highway that connects Westlands to downtown Nairobi, a distance of about one and a half miles. Waiyaki Way was by now experiencing its weekday morning rush hour "traffic jam." Heavy morning traffic included passenger cars, "matatus" (minibuses), and vans, which were heavily packed inside, even with some hanging out both doors. Westlands Lane too was filled with private vehicles, small trucks, and school vans carrying students to school. Pedestrians, who were numerous, could be seen avoiding being "splashed" by insensitive drivers. I had become angry on other occasions by such drivers driving too fast for the potholed road conditions. Human sounds were everywhere of "mafundi" (craftsmen) at work repairing cars, morning radio music and news blaring out from radios positioned in "kiosks." Animated conversations concerning many topics such as inflation, spouses, lovers, and school fees could be heard among travelers proceeding to school, market, workplace, and other destinations. Homes along the road include residential flats and houses, both with gates, usually with an "askari" (house guard) resting at a main gate serving as the entrance to storied buildings or double-storied red-tiled roofed homes, many of the latter owned by Asians. Piles of garbage heaped every several hundred meters along the road were visited regularly by brown dogs, skinny black cats, and poor people, including street children, such as Thomas, all in search of food and/or items for selling. Street boys cannot live only by collecting waste products; they must also scavenge for food and beg. Thomas blended in with other pedestrians also heading to work, many of whom were well dressed in clothes worn for working in Westland's stores and office. Also heading toward Westlands was a small man no taller than a four-year-old child. This elderly man was so terribly deformed that although he could walk, each step was very slow and deliberate. This man was heading to Westlands where he painstakingly goes daily to a strategic location near the post office, a good location for begging, which is his only livelihood. He usually called out to me his greeting as we passed each other every day. He does not greet Thomas when they pass, since they are competitors. Other disabled men are also heading to Westlands this morning as they do daily to occupy their regular street locations where they beg. Some of these people include, among others, a blind man who comes each day by bus to stand near a popular bakery frequented by middle-class Kenyans of all nationalities. A limbless man is carried to his favored spot near an appliance store in front of which he sits on the sidewalk beside his money can. Another man with leg braces, who is also known to me, begs near an Uchumi supermarket store. Some lepers can be found here and there strategically situated where passersby can easily see them. Solitary beggars, such as those mentioned here, tend to be men but not inclusively so. Women, with the exception of lepers, are more likely to be seen begging in groups and often with children. Working street children, like Thomas, who also beg as well as collect paper, constitute the majority of beggars in Nairobi and, as such, sometimes are seen to be a threat by adult beggars who can on occasion, for instance, be heard screaming at street children to clear out of their "territory." (Kilbride field notes, 1995)

BEGGING LOCATIONS

Indeed begging, as we have found in our survey, is a major "survival strategy" for both boys and girls, a strategy that can yield money and tangible things such as food or clothing. As a major source of income, in addition to begging, street girls practice survival sex for money whereas only boys collect *karatasi* as a source of income. Boys are not known to engage in prostitution.

Begging, like other survival strategies among street children, involves strategic locations often with distinct styles of behavior associated with types of territories. Mama Ngina Street, for example, has large international hotels that are frequented by foreign tourists, businesspeople, and wealthy Kenyans, all of whom are potential sources for unusually large sums of money. The Nairobi Hilton Hotel, for instance, is a circular high-rise visible throughout the city. Juxtaposed against this $175 night hotel outpost of the global economy's peripheral geographic margin with its world travelers and their local social class counterparts, less fortunate Kenyans can be seen hurrying and pushing each other for a coveted space to go home aboard one of the diminishing numbers of "stagecoach" buses. Fifteen years ago, such buses totaled over a hundred more than at present even though the population of Nairobi has more than doubled in the same time period. Nowadays, rush hour bus passengers daily brace themselves for a packed journey with fellow travelers heading to one of the city's satellite housing estates or slum areas. For those who cannot afford the modest bus fare of 20 shillings (about 30 cents) "footing" is their daily routine.

Inside the Hilton, costly and repetitive conferences are held, often with international donor support, to once again consider how best to cope with social problems in Nairobi such as congested and terribly potholed streets, diminishing transportation services, and homeless street children, for example. After many years of such repetitive high-level conferences, there is still no evidence of any practical long-term solutions; nor are there any visible outcomes of city planning regarding present or future urban problems. Tourists at the Hilton, including significantly white people who often dress in safari attire for men and casual shorts for women, are escorted in groups at a "safe" distance from the bus stage and other locations where ordinary Kenyans can be found to local game parks to see what for them is "Africa." At the Hilton Hotel, whose interior includes perfumed air conditioning, piped music, CNN in each room, and an international cuisine, some foreign correspondents file stories to Europe and to America concerning "horrors" about neighboring countries in Africa with civil wars, diseases, dictators, street children, and local Kenyan failures of all sorts. Visitors to Kenya rarely venture out of the hotel and almost never take a stagecoach bus to any place in the city. When visitors do explore out from the hotels within Nairobi for other than organized tours inside or outside the city, with the exception of venturesome sorts, they mostly walk along safe and predictable spaces for window shopping, eating, and exercise. These locations and the inclinations of most tourists to fear strangers and to feel sentimentality for less fortunate Kenyans are manipulated by the street children for purposes of begging. For instance, on one occasion, P. K., who was taken to be a tourist, was asked by a small boy for a large sum of money, 100 Kenya shillings, after being sent to him by a woman sitting on the sidewalk. This woman, while holding an infant, was carefully observing the *wazungu* (white people) strolling along, sometimes going to or coming from a popular cinema not far from the Hilton Hotel. The boy's repertoire involves following an appealing passerby with outstretched hands, even for about 50 meters or so, if necessary, all the while "pouting" and asking for help.

Other territories with wealthy visitors and local pedestrians include the City Market in addition to Mama Ngina Street, Kenyatta and Moi Avenues, all with major shopping areas. The International Hotel, which is similar to the Hilton in ambiance and luxurious accommodations, for instance, is an especially favorite begging area for street children and homeless families, who can regularly be seen there. Street girls begging, often with babies on their backs to attract sympathy, are particularly prevalent at such lucrative locations. Some street girls believe that babies are likely to attract large sums of money from tourists in particular. For example, P. K., once again taken to be a tourist, was frequently asked at all of these locations to "help the baby."

BEGGING STYLES

As we report in this chapter, we discovered in our survey research that begging is an important means of income for both street boys and girls. In our ethnographic work, begging was discovered to have patterned styles of behavior learned by the children for success. In begging, verbal requests for specific things are not uncommon. Street boys have been observed pointing in the direction of a shoe store or a bakery, for example, while asking people to "buy me shoes" or "buy me bread." Begging styles typically include not only verbal requests but also holding a hand out, pouting, exaggerated smiling, and, less frequently, threatening gestures with face and hands. For instance, on one occasion P. K., while walking near a park lined with food places, was joined in stride by a street boy who while walking beside him, but with no eye contact, said over and over again "ten shillings" in slowly rising speech that ended in a shouted request. Afterwards, when the request was not successful, the street boy matter-of-factly joined several other boys in rummaging through a garbage can in front of a chicken and chips fastfood place.

Our observations have revealed that street children successfully beg from a full range of givers although *wazungu* are thought by them to be the most likely source for large sums. In Westlands we have observed that boys generally and consistently receive the most money by begging from white men and women in cars, on motorcycles, or from passersby walking along the sidewalks. Asian and African Kenyans (and visitors) of all ethnicities also have been observed giving money and food. Givers reveal a variety of emotions when giving, such as fear (rapid raising of car windows, for example), pity, and amused disinterest, all of which have been repeatedly observed by us.

Street boys report that children can beg up to the age of 14 years, when they no longer look "innocent" or when they start to feel "ashamed." Some boys report that they sniff glue so as to get courage to beg. Although both boys and girls can be seen begging, some older street girls report feeling uncomfortable in doing so because in some situations the begging behavior may carry a sexual connotation among members of the public. For girls, begging can be a risky survival strategy. The police routinely target street children for a variety of reasons, but especially for begging. We have observed street boys in Westlands being grabbed by police and taken off to jail because, according to the police, begging "disturbs people." Some street children have confided to us their fear that the food they are given by some of their benefactors may contain poison, a fear of considerable importance now that many people no longer give money but only food, since it is now known, as we shall see, to be common for street boys to exchange money for glue instead of using the requested money for food or clothing.

OCCUPATIONAL STREET SPACE

Although most street children at one time or another beg, a common public stereotype that this is their *only* attempt at getting money is untrue. In fact, street boys in particular participate in an occupational street space that is complex and varied. Prolonged observation of a busy street favored at lunchtime by street boys in Westlands, for instance, reveals a complexity of shared street space for gaining a livelihood. Seated on the pavement beside one another along a main street, as well as along other streets, are shoeshine vendors and newspaper sellers. Walking about on the sidewalk and street are flower sellers and hawkers of radios, watches, flashlights, telephones, dust pans, magazines, fruits, and vegetables. This street, as do others, has stalls with used clothes for sale and kiosks where fruits and vegetables are sold. Seen among all of this occupational activity are crippled adults and street children begging. While standing amongst taxi drivers anxiously hailing potential customers, street boys attempt to earn money by guarding or washing parked cars. All of these people and products are accessible to the public, either on foot or from inside a passenger vehicle. Shops in buildings line the street too but can be accessed only by foot.

The observer is also struck not only by how the street child blends in with other street workers but also by the social complexity characterizing members of the general public going about their business among whom the street child is almost imperceptible. The streets reveal spoken sounds of Kikuyu, Luo, Gujurati, Kiswahili, English, French, *sheng* ("slang" spoken by street children and most youths in urban Kenya), and other languages heard against the backdrop of street noises such as horns, racing engines, screeching tires, and so on. Sights of people of various shades of brown and black with hair short, plaited, braided, or beneath wigs and sights of colorfully dressed people wearing school uniforms, skirts, *kanzus* (long white robes), *fezzes* (hats), jeans, multiemblemed sweat shirts, sandals, high-heeled shoes, and barefoot are in sharp contrast to white tourists dressed in shorts and safari (trip) attire. The senses are attacked by both unpleasant and pleasant street smells such as exhaust fumes, city council toilets, cooked foods, garbage, roses, fried chicken, and fresh fruits.

Amidst the diverse sights, sounds and smells, some of which are described here, various street boys can be seen not only begging but working at *karatasi* collection or earning occasional money by washing cars or by working as an *askari* (guard) at night at a kiosk. Some boys can be observed where cars are parked working as "parking boys," which involves guiding the parking of cars, guarding them, and feeding parking meters (before these were removed) if necessary. For most members of the public, especially foreign observers, there is little awareness of the social complexity of occupational street space inhabited by street children. Rather, it is only their begging and the glue bottle that serve for the visitor as a clear symbolic marker of street child identity, symbols that often prevent the casual or unfamiliar observer's gaze from even noticing the solitary street child such as Thomas who, without a glue bottle is, in fact, a working street child. Like most other Kenyans on the streets, he sets off in the morning to work, in his case, by collecting *karatasi* and by begging along the way if an opportunity arises.

When family conditions deteriorate because of increasing poverty, some needy children from the slum communities turn to the streets to earn a living. Some 54% of the children in our survey were living on the streets fulltime. Many of them reported, however, that they had maintained contact with their families. Another 46% were going home regularly and coming from home every morning to work on the streets. The survey reveals that 47% of the children had been on the streets for over two years. A further 25% had lived on the streets for a year. The average period of time on the street was 2.6 years.

Virtually all the children in the sample (99%) were engaged in some form of activity to earn an income. The most common types of work were begging (about 46%) and collecting waste paper and scrap metals (about 32.2%). Table 6.1 shows the range of the children's main work on the street as they reported them.

Table 6.1
Children's Major Occupations on the Street

Major Occupations	N	%
Begging	183	45.7
Collecting waste paper & scrap metal	129	32.3
Cleaning vehicles	24	6.0
Selling groundnuts	24	6.0
Carrying goods for customers at stores/markets	23	5.8
Watching parked vehicles	8	2.0
Selling charcoal	5	1.2
Roasting maize for sale	4	1.0
Total	400	100.0

As shown in this table, the children in the sample were involved in various kinds of work including hawking, begging, watching and cleaning parked cars, collecting waste paper, bottles, cans, and anything they could get and sell from garbage heaps. They do this in order to raise some money for themselves and their families. Most of the street children found around Kenyatta Market, for example, are involved in washing and guarding cars for people who have gone to shop or to purchase roast meat in the market. The children who collect and sell waste papers were mainly found and interviewed around Gomongo and Dagoretti corner, where the city commission dumps garbage. Children selling groundnuts were mostly found near Muthurwa. Most of these children come from around Muthurwa, Makongeni, Kaloleni, and the surrounding residential areas. The majority of them told us that they were out of school and had been asked by their parents to sell groundnuts and fruits by the roadside to supplement their family incomes. As many as 60% of the children said that they give some of their earnings to their families while the remaining 40% said they keep their incomes for themselves. Our observations revealed that some of the children earned their living through prostitution and the sale of drugs although these illicit types of occupations were not explicitly reported by the children themselves, but could be inferred from their responses. The majority of the children (95%) were not employed by anyone, but were doing their own work. Unfortunately they are frequently exploited by unscrupulous middlemen and women who buy waste papers and other scrap materials from them. There are exceptions to this exploitation, however, as we will see in the material on "Mama Ford" in the next chapter. The children worked long hours to raise a few shillings. Most of them are overworked and underpaid. The majority of them (58.4%) reported that they worked for 10 hours and over. The average daily working hours was 9.4. Viewed against their age, it appears that their economic pursuits and their struggle for survival had left them with much less time to play and to enjoy their childhood. The number of hours worked in a day is presented in Table 6.2.

Table 6.2
Number of Hours Children Worked in a Day

Hours	N	%
4	2	0.5
5	8	2.0
6	19	4.8
7	27	6.8
8	70	17.5
9	40	10.0
10	160	40.0
11	13	3.3
12	56	14.0
13	5	1.1
Total	400	100.0

Considering the fact that most street children may not have received adequate family support and that many of them likely have been abused, abandoned, or neglected by their parents or guardians, group formation and mutual support were critical to their survival. When asked whether they do their work alone or in a group with other street children, 93% said they work in a group. There was some division of labor, though not rigidly maintained, based on age and gender.

Broadly, there are two main reasons for working in a group. One reason is economic. In order to be successful in their work such as begging and washing cars, for instance, the children needed to plan their strategies and operations together. This is one of the survival techniques they had learned in order to deal with the challenges of street life. The second reason is social and psychological. Like everyone else, these children need friendship. And like the *camadas* of Cali in Colombia described in Lewis Aptekar's study (1988, pp. 120–121), most of the street children in our sample (88%) moved and worked in a group for purposes of friendship and mutual support. The peer support that they receive from one another by caring and sharing is not only a substitute for what they needed and missed from their own families but is also psychologically gratifying. The social networks developed through friendship make them more psychologically prepared to cope with the insecurities of street life.

Some of the most difficult information to verify is people's income, particularly for those who work outside the formal wage sector. The street children were no exception. Although these children do make some shillings, most of them live from hand to mouth, which makes it difficult to know the total collection at the end of a working day. We were able to get more specific daily income information for a small number of children through ethnographic work in Westlands. In addition, many children in the sample not only saw us as potential benefactors but also expected some payment for their time and information. Thus, answers to the questions on their incomes were certainly suspected to be influenced by their perceptions or expectations of the potential benefits. Whatever the amount of money they said they were getting from their work in a day or a month depended, to some extent, on what they expected from us. Such cunningness is part of their art of survival.

Seventy-seven percent of the children in our survey were getting 20–40 Kenya shillings (between 30 and 80 cents) in a day. The highest amount reported was 150 shillings a day, and the average daily income was 34 shillings. Most of them got an estimated monthly income of 500 shillings. There were some inconsistencies in reporting daily and monthly incomes, so the figures given by the children were nothing more than estimates based on their recollections. Nevertheless, it was clear to us that incomes were quite meager.

The majority of the children (71%) said they spent most of their money on food. Another 17% reported that they took all their earnings to their mothers to supplement the family income. The others said they used their money to buy clothes (7%) or glue (3%) and to pay rent (2%). The survey results in Table 6.3 show what the children said they like most about their work.

The thing that the children said they liked most about their work is the money (83%). Only 7% liked the free food left over from the kiosks, restaurants, and hotels in Nairobi, and places near where they worked. Another 6% said they did not like anything about their work, while only 4% liked the freedom in the streets that was made possible by working there.

Table 6.3
What the Street Children Like Most about Their Work

What They Liked Most	N	%
Money	332	83.0
Free food	28	7.0
Freedom	16	4.0
Nothing	24	6.0
Total	400	100.0

The children reported to us that working on the streets exposed them to a wide range of problems.   The major difficulties experienced by the street children during the course of their work included harassment by the police, lack of food, scarcity of waste papers and low prices for them, theft among themselves, lack of sleeping places, and lack of sympathy from the public.

Chapter 7

Community Life and Social Organization of Street Children

It was mid-afternoon when I suggested to a key informant that we should proceed to an excellent confectionery in Westlands, a place where I could enjoy Kenyan coffee and an apple tart or other sweet cake.   This establishment catered to some tourists, Kenyan Asians, and African Kenyans who shared with me a sweet tooth.   Daniel listened to me while continuing his remarks on why he had become a street boy several years earlier.   He was a frequent companion of mine who was an excellent participant in what for me was an ongoing exercise in dialogic methodology, informal conversations in order to obtain his verbal "discourse" about his perceived social reality.   Nevertheless, research methodology and the pleasures of dialogue aside, visions of apple tart or even better, apple pies won out over dialogue, and I pressed his preference to "take a break."   Visiting the confectionery would also enable me to offer tea, meat pies, or sausage to Daniel, who did not have my sweet tooth. Daniel had not enjoyed the affluence prerequisite to the acquisition of expensive sweets made of processed sugar.   He, like many Kenyans who do not regularly eat or drink sweets, has never been to a dentist nor in his sixteen years has he ever had a dental cavity (other street children had, however, reported suffering from toothache).   Just before entering the confectionery, Daniel stopped in his tracks and stepped aside to let me enter. Surprised, I also stopped and asked Daniel what was the problem. He responded, "I can't go in unless I go and buy new clothes.   Otherwise they will know that I am a street boy."   I answered that he looked fine in his clean trousers, shirt, and shoes. Nevertheless, Daniel refused to enter a social space where "he did not belong." (Kilbride field notes, 1995)

Street children relate to the public somewhat differently in diverse communities throughout Nairobi. For example, the children of Westlands have developed a community structure, work routines, and survival strategies based on the presence of relatively affluent Kenyans and visitors as well as on the availability of an abundant and steady source of waste products. Children come to Westlands from elsewhere. Another niche involving a somewhat different adaptive strategy characterizes those children living in Mukuru-Reuben, a somewhat rural-like location in the city where street children are of the community and are rehabilitated there through a program sponsored by Feed the Children, an NGO. Street children residing at this community youth center have consistent interaction with family members who live in the community. Street children begging and sleeping near the large tourist locations have developed begging styles described previously including tactics designed to appeal to the tourists. Street girls tend to reside near the city market where there is a clustering of available water and food sources, people to beg from, and nightspots for survival sex.

Regardless of where they live in Nairobi, the street child can be said to be at the bottom of a status hierarchy that is sharply delineated in Kenyan society as our example of Daniel shows. As was described in chapter 4, affluent suburbs with large gated homes, multiple cars, servants, trips abroad all stand in sharp contrast to slums where hundreds of thousands of "squatters" are crowded into areas with no sewage, proper sanitation, clean and safe drinking water, permanent houses, or electricity. Social class distinctions compete with ethnic affiliation to divide Kenyans into distinct, often antagonistic, social categories. At the bottom of the national status hierarchy the street child increasingly serves as a stigmatized symbol of class antagonism for both wealthy and working-class Kenyans. The latter reside in numerous suburban housing estates where a regular salary is a prerequisite for house rent or ownership but not enough to purchase the symbols of wealth such as education abroad for one's children, shopping trips or holidays to Europe, international credit cards, and many other things beyond the means of most Kenyans, except for the richest.

Daniel, like many other street children, is aware of class antagonism toward them, most directly in the form of police harassment but also experienced as fear of poisoning from members of the public who give them gifts of food. Children note, too, the hasty retreats usually made by fearful people in such acts as moving away from them while seated on buses and rapidly rolling up car windows in their presence. Interestingly, some street children have commented to us that their own community operates, for the most part, free of sharp social distinctions, especially ethnic antagonism. Their remarks are in agreement with our own observations that although street children are separated by age and gender distinctions, as compared to adults, there is little evidence of ethnic animosity in their work, friendship, sleeping arrangements, or other social interactions. This observation pertains to boys. It is our impression that a Kikuyu ethnicity predominates among girls compared to boys, among whom ethnic groups are more varied.   This suggests also that boys travel longer distances to reach Nairobi than do girls inasmuch as the Kikuyu are the Nairobi region's largest ethnic group.   Others have also noted in Africa a minimal amount of ethnic tension among street boys.   Writing about Sudan, Cole Dodge and Magne Raundalen (1991) state, "groups of street children in Khartoum comprised members from all areas, all religions, speaking different languages from diverse tribes.   The groups functioned well together, in stark contrast to Sudanese society as a whole" (p. 47).

Perhaps group solidarity is enhanced by a strong negative opinion held by the public concerning street children.   Our field research assistant, Michael, was interviewed about public reaction to street children whom he had observed in the course of our study of street children in their social environment.   He feels that some people seem annoyed when they are approached by begging children.   Others fear to walk near or to pass by street children as they regard them as pickpockets and thieves.   Some adults confront the children and ask them why they are on the streets, since they are sent there, they believe, by their parents.   Some people told Michael that street children should be arrested, having in their view mainly escaped from jails as criminals.   One man told him, "The street children are the most dangerous people in the society as they take a lot of drugs.   They can steal from or even kill innocent people."   Some people consider street children to be sinners who need prayers from members of the public.   Michael once observed a street boy picking up a discarded mango thrown away by a kiosk grocer who, while chasing the boy away, yelled that he was the one who brought flies around.   On another occasion, a street boy riding a bus happened to sit near a well-dressed woman.   The boy dressed in rags occasioned the woman to leave her seat, which was then taken by a man.   Michael also talked to members of the public who felt sympathetic about street children as less fortunate children in need of help.   Overall, however, the prevailing public view is one of fear, stigma, and avoidance.

HUSBANDS AND WIVES

The idiom of marriage is used to characterize long-term, committed relationships between street children and their mates.   The term "husband and wife" is used frequently by partners and others to refer to relationships that result in children whom both partners recognize or to a friendship that involves committed sexual relations.   Many husband and wife ties involve street boys and street girls although both frequently have familial-like conjugal relationships with people other than street children.   Some girls from Jevanjee Gardens, for example, have or have had husband ties with boys from Westlands.   Wanjiru, whose life we profile in chapter 8, is one example.   Margaret also has had a "husband" who was a pickpocket but not a street boy.   Westland boys, in addition to having permanent girlfriends from Jevanjee Gardens and elsewhere, also develop husband and wife ties with girls on and off the streets.   One such case is Wamzee, a boy who over the years we knew him experienced an improvement in his economic condition, a situation that seemingly contributed to his appeal to a late adolescent girl living in Kangemi.

For some boys in Westlands, a relationship may involve having a child subsequent to which the parents consider themselves to be married. Papa, a street boy we had known for five years, had acquired in 1999 a newfound sense of family responsibility for his six-month-old baby. His wife knows about his past life as a street boy. By now, in his late twenties, he is preoccupied with making money for his family. He is a "transporter" of vegetables to market and assists women in transporting their vegetables from the street to their kiosks in the Westlands market. Papa declined P. K.'s invitation to lunch in favor of some money for his wife and baby. He said, "I will eat at home with them." Currently, Papa no longer sleeps in Westlands. He lives in a slum location where he was given permission by the chief there to build a house. His work aspiration now is to acquire a personal wagon to assist him in his job as a transporter. Papa described another former street boy known to us who now has a baby and is currently applying for a car wash license to enhance his ability to support his wife and their infant.

WAMZEE AND SUSAN

We first met Wamzee in 1994 when he was about 16 years old and sleeping at Sabaima, a sleeping place described in chapter 8, while working regularly as a collector of paper. Originally from Machakos, Wamzee is a Muslim who went as far as standard 7 (7th grade). His nature is low key with a somewhat cheery disposition, and he is very fond of his pet dog. His physique is slender, and he is of medium height. He smiles often but has poor teeth. Wamzee is thought by some to be a source for glue and other substances. Nevertheless, over the four years of our acquaintance, Wamzee devoted a considerable amount of effort to collecting paper. Because of his age and strength, Wamzee is able to collect paper in bulk. He has ties with *askaris* (guards) who allow him to collect large bundles on a regular basis. On many days Wamzee is able to collect 70 kilos a day that he sold in 1994 to a middle person called Mama Ford for 210 shillings (about $3). Wamzee estimated that of this amount he spent about 106 shillings a day for food, 20 shillings for cigarettes, 14 shillings for bus transport to Kangemi for visits, and 20 shillings on friends, leaving him with the balance of 50 shillings for "pocket money." He uses his pocket money to visit Machakos or saves it for future needs. Wamzee considers himself to be a *chokora* because he collects paper. He, however, buys or cooks only good food and differentiates himself from other street boys, such as Jacob (see chapter 8), who are *chokora kwa chakula* (a boy who collects waste food from dustbins). Jacob, younger and not as strong as Wamzee, earns fewer than 50 shillings a day from his paper collecting, not enough to sustain himself without eating waste food. There is, therefore, an incipient social class structure among street children based not only on age but also on income.

One of the advantages of a good income is an opportunity for pocket money. By 1996, with the help of a charitable organization, Wamzee had moved from Sabaima into a small kiosk area near the main Westlands roundabout where he was able to sleep and get donated food for himself and other street children. He also sold items like *miraa* (a drug), bread, and cigarettes. Now Wamzee was earning more money than he had by paper collecting previously. While talking with Wamzee at his kiosk one day in 1997, P. K. noticed a wedding band on his finger and asked about it. He agreed to bring his "wife" Susan to meet P. K., and subsequently we interviewed Wamzee and Susan about their relationship. Susan spoke excellent English, but since Wamzee did not, we decided to do the interview in Kiswahili by a research assistant and without P. K. being present to promote informality. Susan was a superb informant. Then in her late teens (19), she lives with her parents in Kangemi. Susan, although a Protestant, is the same ethnic group as Wamzee, a Kamba. She is quiet, attractive, dresses well, has been to standard 8 in primary school but does not presently work. Susan also wears a gold-colored wedding ring matching Wamzee's. Our interview revealed the following information about their relationship.

A few months prior to our interivew, Wamzee and Susan first met at Susan's home in Kangemi. He had gone there with a friend when he first saw Susan coming home from a shop. The next day, Wamzee sent his friend to see Susan on his behalf. Susan, who once worked in a shop in Westlands, has a child by a previous relationship. Although they do not use family planning, they do not want children, as they are not yet formally married. Susan says she comes to see Wamzee nearly every day. Similarly, Wamzee goes regularly to Kangemi to meet Susan there, often in the morning. Wamzee bought her a gold ring and gave it to her in Kangemi. When asked about the ring, Wamzee said, "She knows very well why she is wearing it on the third finger which means she has not wedded. In two years' time, she will have transferred the ring to the other finger to mean she is married." Susan added, "Wamzee bought the ring for me because he is now like my husband." Wamzee said his own ring on his finger is "for love" because Susan gave it to him. Wamzee was happy the day they began to wear their rings together. He said that he was waiting for the year to end, as they would then marry. Susan laughingly said that Wamzee should give her several months' notice if that is the case. Wamzee agreed, saying time was needed to inform her parents and also to visit her home near Machakos (Ukambani). Susan's parents already know about Wamzee, but she does not yet know Wamzee's home area. Susan continued, "The first time Wamzee came to our place, he found both my parents in the house. I was sleeping. He was asked what brought him there. He said he was looking for me. My mother woke me up to greet my visitor. I was scared to see him in front of my parents. When I saw him off, my mother asked me about him. I said he was my boyfriend, and she did nothing."

Susan and Wamzee are now on intimate emotional terms. Few people, for example, know Wamzee's real name. Susan does not address him by his nickname, Wamzee, but only by his real name. They wear matching rings and use "love talk" when in each other's company. Still, not all of Wamzee's friends know about Susan, and her parents are not aware that she regularly visits Wamzee in Westlands. The idiom of marriage is blended in their conversation with ideal requirements of courtship patterns in the wider society (e.g., meeting the parents, planning to wed). The marriage ideal of contemporary Kenya, as yet unfulfilled, was at the forefront of their conversations with us about themselves.

SIBLINGS

There are sibling relationships among some of the street children, but this relationship is not as salient as previously in Kenya or even today in most families. Our informants know of examples of sibling ties, but generally siblings tend to live apart while on the streets. On occasion, a person will recruit his or her sibling, or a child will seek out a sibling known to be on the streets. One girl in Jevanjee Gardens, for example, left home after her parents died, and there was no money. She looked for and found on the streets her sister, who then helped her get adjusted. Jacob, mentioned earlier and who is profiled later in chapter 8, had a younger brother on the streets in Westlands, one who was sent away to school. This brother, after leaving school in standard 7, followed Jacob to Westlands. He came to the streets because "I was convinced by my brother, Jacob, that life on the streets is not as hard as the one I was leading at home." Jacob and his brother never ate or slept together while on the streets. This was because Jacob is a paper collector and his brother not. They help each other when sick and never fight together, according to Jacob's brother. We know of other cases of older brothers and sisters caring for younger siblings of both genders.

In the summer of 1994, Bryn Mawr College student A. Rhae Adams looked specifically at sibling relationships among street children. Working in Nairobi with a Kenyan ethnographic assistant from the Maryknoll Institute of African Studies, Adams summarizes her conclusions as follows:

Some children, while not being in any way biologically related, established themselves as sibling pairs on the streets. One such pair was Mary and Joseph. They moved as a team and shared territory. This may be the reason they considered each other family. They may have begun by sharing an area of the city and developed a relationship out of this. However, this labeling was not consistent. Some days they would refer to each other as sister and brother, some days not. Regardless of this, though, they still acted towards one another as if they felt such a relation. They exhibited some of the same behaviors as consanguine sibling pairs such as watching over each other, sharing, and teamwork in begging. Additionally, some of the older children, while not using the sibling relation terms with other children, exhibit behaviors such as watching over the younger ones. (Adams, 1994, pseudonyms used)

The use of "fictive" sibling kin terms socially constructed among street children serves to resemble biologically based interdependent family relations in the wider Kenyan society. A similar social invention of nonbiologically based family relationships has been documented in other social situations where exclusion from conventional kinship ties have resulted from stigma and marginalization (see Weston, 1991). Adams noted that when sibling relations are disconnected, stressful circumstances can result. She writes:

When Robert was around and sober, he was an attentive older brother. He ensured Jane had her fair share of any food or money that was being handed out, and that she was "safe" from danger. However, when he was high from sniffing glue, he could not even tell me where she was, in fact, he had trouble remembering who she was. One of the effects of the narcotic, then, was to break down a sibling support system upon which an eight year-old girl, with essentially no home and no other family, counted. (Adams, 1994, pseudonyms used)

It should be noted concerning sibling relationships that all of our ethnographic research was undertaken among street children who were migrants. We have observed, however, street children families of brothers and sisters born on the streets. Among these families of street children, sibling ties are salient. In begging, for example, we have observed older siblings carrying younger ones on their backs to beg and also minding their siblings while at rest.

FUNERALS

Without doubt, the most significant social ritual in many indigenous cultures and still widely practiced today is the funeral. A proper burial by one's kinsfolk, ideally in a rural homeland, is at the forefront of symbolic significance of extended family values. A Nairobi court case concerning burial customs and changing family values aptly illustrates, for example, the cultural significance of burial ritual among the Luo of western Kenya. This case concerned the rights of a widow to bury her husband in Nairobi against the claims of his Luo clan to bury him in western Kenya. The fact that his clan, instead of his widow, was awarded custody over the deceased's body illustrates clan power and ethnic identity. Where one's body and spirit are to be buried is a key symbol of identity, since one's place of burial is what Luo consider their home. In January 1987, the nation of Kenya was captivated by this dramatic court case brought about by the death of a prominent Nairobi-based attorney named Otieno. From the *Daily Nation* as quoted in Sean Egan (1987), we learn:

He was a Luo by tribe, educated in Nakesene and India and had a very substantial and varied legal practice in Nairobi. He married the plaintiff, a Kikuyu lady of one of

Kenya's leading Kikuyu families, and numbered among his clients people of all tribes and races. He was a metropolitan and a cosmopolitan, and though he undoubtedly honored the tradition of his ancestors, it is hard to envisage such a person as subject to African customary law and in particular to the custom of a rural community (p. 6).

While Otieno's body remained in the mortuary, the courts deliberated. Thousands of his clansmen and others favorable to his wife waited around the court chamber on a daily basis. Sometimes it required tanks to control the crowd. In the words of the *Daily Nation*, as cited by Egan (1987), the Otieno episode

raised many issues of wide interest to many people. The role of the law and the family, customary law versus common law, the role of women in the family, different ethnic traditions and their place in Kenya society as a whole. The whole issue evoked strong feelings, emotions, and debate. For newspapers it was a bestseller. For let there be no mistake about it, Otieno's case may be closed but the debate it gave rise to about many issues has only just begun (p. 7).

So culturally significant is the funeral in the Luo imagination that children of both sexes frequently imitate funeral ceremonies in their play (see Ominde, 1952, p. 13). Burials are socially significant for Kenyans of both sexes in those societies, which have elaborate burial observances. Burials are frequently events where social and cultural issues emerge over inheritance claims, for example, and are contested and sometimes resolved (M. Cattell, personal communication). Many street boys participate in the funeral rituals for family members, when possible, and for fellow street children on a regular basis. Among the boys in Westlands, one of our most frequent requests for money came in the form of requests for funds to go home to attend funerals. Both boys and girls participate in funerals held for fellow street children.

Daniel described a recent funeral that is typical of those encountered among street children. He gave the following account, which we have translated into standard English,

On a recent holiday my two friends went to Kangemi and came back to Westlands drunk. One friend, Rasta, was sleeping near the bus stage where buses and *matatus* are heavy. We carried him to my place. Ochieng, however, was also drunk and started acting like a "tout" (collector of fees for *matatu* drivers) calling people to enter a *matatu*. After it was full, Ochieng also entered the *matatu* but as we approached, he was thrown out of it, was injured, and he died. All of us street kids went mad, running here and there. We gave the *matatu* number and name (Queen of Sheba) to the police. The priest came and calmed us down. He prevented us from burning the *matatu*. It started to rain and the police allowed us to carry Ochieng's body to the police car after the priest gave last rites. Two boys, Papa one of them, went with the police car to the city mortuary. Some of us went to the mortuary with the priest. We all carried the body into the mortuary after the police made us clean blood from their car. The next day while we sat around our fire, we saw the *matatu* so we went to the bus stage. We picked stones to throw at the *matatu*, but the driver said he wasn't the driver yesterday. The owner was in the *matatu* and the police after calming us down ordered them to drive to the police station. We went also and wrote our statement. The police asked us about Ochieng's relatives. We said they live in Tanzania. The police gave us a funeral permit so we could collect money so as to announce Ochieng's death on the Tanzanian radio. In eleven days we collected 13,000 shillings in donations from street kids and the public. The priest went to Tanzania and returned with Ochieng's parents while we stayed to collect money. After some days we had collected 22,000 shillings. The priest contributed thousands of shillings too. Ochieng's relatives also contributed. We hired a *matatu* to take us to Tanzania. We also gave Ochieng's father money for a coffin and bought clothes for the funeral. Many of us left by a rented Nissan van for Tanzania. We accompanied the body. Once there, we found many "grandmothers" (relatives) waiting. When they saw the body, they started wailing. We took the body to Ochieng's father's house. A tent was built for us. We were given food (fish and porridge). As his friends, we were asked to dig the grave. As a Luo, Ochieng had to have a grave dug after midnight, so we did that. By 5:00 A.M. we had finished the grave. Amidst singing, we buried Ochieng in his coffin, which we carried to the grave. His parents threw sand in the grave, and he was buried. We put flowers on the grave and then returned to the house and were given meat. We then returned to Nairobi.

Participation in funerals is one social mechanism whereby boys in Westlands remain linked to conventional society. Death and grief overrides for most people the special stigmatized status that street children regularly endure.

SLEEPING ARRANGEMENTS

During the day, community life for the street child blends with other poor people for whom the street is also a vital means of livelihood. Street jobs are sometimes called *jua kali* which is a Kiswahili term for "hot sun," an economy made up of workers who are primarily outdoors and unlicensed. Street children themselves, as we have seen in the focus group material, do have a strong sense of what distinctively defines a street child. Nevertheless, some informants point out in informal discussions that they are really little different from other working poor with whom they have daytime interactions on the street. *Jua kali* workers too face many economic insecurities and even periodic harassment by city council *askaris* in such acts as tearing down their unlicensed kiosks. In fact, some street boys wonder whether or not there is really a qualitative difference between sleeping in a *chuom* (temporary structure made of paper and cardboards) or in a slum house, lacking as it does in ventilation and having leaky roofs and walls. Others disagree, however, pointing out that at least a slum home provides protection from the police and cold weather. What primarily distinguishes street children from the working poor are evening activities, including sleeping outdoors.

Many street children sleep away from their parents although this is a practice common in indigenous cultures as we have noted. Like their indigenous counterparts, street children also sleep in groups, rarely alone except for older boys who sometimes do so. Street boys, for instance, regularly sleep with age cohorts, and those who beg together or collect paper together tend to sleep together, too. Ties of friendship also serve as a basis for sleeping arrangements. Frequent movement to new sleeping locations is common for both boys and girls, often in response to actual or anticipated roundups by the police. Community social life can be observed in Westlands, for example, at night around fires while the boys converse, warm their food, or lounge about before sleeping. When the weather is cold in July and August, the fires provide warmth, too. One 16 year-old boy regularly sleeps at the main Westlands roundabout with about seven companions. When it rains, they sleep inside in a small house near the roundabout. The house's owner, a woman, gives them accommodation free of charge on condition that when they wake up, they must clean her place in preparation for selling used clothing. At morning, each boy sets out to secure his own breakfast. Before sleeping at the roundabout, some of the boys used to sleep at another popular sleeping location, Sabaima, but they were chased away by nearby kiosk owners who believed that one of them, Daniel, who was jailed, was stealing eggs from them to be resold for money.

Children commonly report difficulties in sleeping at night. Inclement weather, fear of police harassment, attacks by fellow street boys, especially of street girls, are frequent complaints. On this point, Haverford College student Vera Limcuando wrote about her ethnographic observations undertaken with her Maryknoll Institute of African Studies research assistant in 1994 as follows:

The boys told me of their fears as they lived on the streets. Many said they were burdened by the cold and the older boys who would sometimes steal from them in their sleep. Apparently the street children sleep wherever they fall from exhaustion, but most like to settle in a place which they feel is most safe. Kiilu told me that he stayed near the Kenya cinema where he could pay a watchman to keep guard over him and his few possessions as he slept. I found it very disturbing to learn that a boy who barely has enough money to eat has to spend some of his earnings on protection from the older boys in the street. The other boys talked of their fears in the night. They were burdened by the cold, the mosquitoes, and the hunger. The boys simply sleep in the same clothes they had worn all day and the previous few days. They used newspapers as blankets and literally slept in the alleyways or sidewalks. None of them ever went to sleep feeling safe. (Limcuando, 1994, pseudonym used)

Street girls fear rape at night in addition to stresses reported by boys. In fact, street girls often sleep during the day so that they may be awake at night to avoid rape attempts and also to work at survival sex, which occurs primarily at night. Collette Suda, in her survey, noted difficulties in getting female respondents during the day.

A Westlands street boy, Daniel, and P. K. worked together to obtain evening census information from sleeping areas in Westlands. While Daniel was away, P. K. undertook spot observations and informal interviews to compare with data collected alone by Daniel. Daniel gathered evening census material during the first week of August 1995, the cool season. In general, at this time, girls were only seen sleeping in Westlands on the one day a week when food was given out by a charitable organization. On this day, children came from miles away to get food or perhaps also to socialize and otherwise enjoy reading lessons and songs provided along with the food. The day before feeding there were no girls sleeping at Sabaima or the main roundabout where there were 9 boys and 40 boys, respectively. There were 66 boys and 6 girls sleeping at these two locations the night of the feeding, compared to only 39 boys the night after the feeding. On Saturdays, the boys stay out much later than on weeknights. For instance, one boy, while observed resting on Sunday, commented, "We are doing nothing as today is Sunday." Boys play games, wash clothes, and take baths on Sundays. There is also a concern to find food on Sundays, since charitable organizations tend to operate during the week only.

One weekday evening in the second week of August at 9:00 P.M. during one spot observation, P. K. was taken by two street boys around Westlands to check on sleeping patterns. Daniel was out of town at this time. The spot observation confirmed information we obtained through census count and informal interviews. We quote from the spot observations made at the four major sleeping locations:

Sabaima 9:00 P.M.: 8 boys are around a fire. Mcoasti called to me and we chatted. Mrefu was there, too. They brought me to see Jacob, who was asleep near the fire. He was under wraps asleep with 5 other younger boys. 7 boys will sleep here tonight. Mcoasti will not. 2 boys are older.
Main Island Roundabout 9:20 P.M.: 14 boys are having tea near the roundabout. All are small boys. All will sleep at the roundabout. No children are there yet.
Westview 9:30 P.M.: 6 boys, including Mcoasti, who has just arrived, will sleep here tonight. Mcoasti showed me a bag of trash that he will use as a pillow. Mixed older and younger boys are here.
Jacaranda 9:45 P.M.: I greeted Wamzee, Papa, and Almonde. These 3 older boys will sleep here tonight.

These spot checks revealed that by 9:45 P.M., only boys and no girls were distributed across four main sleeping areas, with age as a significant variable. Some sleeping groups are mixed by age. Others have primarily younger (under 14) or older (late teens) boys. Eleven of these boys were asleep by 9:30 P.M. although all the older boys were awake.

CONFLICT

While clearly the targets of widespread public antagonism based on class, it is our impression that street children have in recent years entered into growing conflict with those with whom they share the street as an occupational space. Recent media accounts, for example, report a recurring number of cases of violence involving street boys and their immediate working neighbors on the streets. For example, one street boy was stoned to death by 10 hawkers for "stealing a sweet." In another violent incident, 200 street boys went on a car smashing rampage after which angry *matatu* drivers killed a street boy. About 100 street boys protested this killing and demanded the arrest of the driver. It is felt by some boys that sometimes *matatu* drivers intentionally run them down. Another case involves street boys and night watchmen, which saw one street boy and a watchman dead and several others hospitalized in critical condition. In our own personal observation noted earlier, one "green grocer" was seen chasing a street boy away because "he brought flies," reflecting a common belief among grocers that street boys are "dirty." In cases of theft from Westland's kiosks, street boys are among the first to be accused, and in one instance a boy was arrested for stealing eggs despite claims of innocence.

To date, street girls seem not to have experienced as many daytime overtly violent encounters as boys with other poor Kenyans. This is so mainly because their primary economic strategy along with begging is survival sex, which means that they work mainly at night. Nevertheless, as we shall see later, violence is a routine aspect for those girls involved in survival sex, often at the hands of night watchmen, street boys, and/or wealthy men of all races. Since street boy violence occurs during the daytime, it is often reported to the press, unlike the more private episodes of violence suffered by girls alone at night. Nevertheless, girls are regularly victimized by police. By virtue of their position at the bottom of the status hierarchy involving both street girls and boys, girls often become victims of violence inflicted on them by street boys.

MAMA FORD

Survival through work is a significant activity for street boys, as we have noted elsewhere. A fixture in the social organization and economic survival of the street boys who live in Westlands is a woman known by the street boys as "Mama Ford." Her nickname derives from her support of the political party FORD (Forum for the Restoration of Democracy). This woman is a hard-working person in her 40s who has managed to support her own children through higher education including the University of Nairobi. Mama Ford spends a great deal of time every day adjacent to the Sabaima sleeping location receiving, weighing, and paying out money for *karatasi* purchased from street boys living and working in Westlands. She is well liked by the boys, who speak fondly about her. Through her several years working closely with the street boys, she has become very knowledgeable about their circumstances, community social organization, and personalities. In 1995, P. K. had interviews with her that were followed by informal discussions in subsequent years. What follows is an extended commentary reported to us by Mama Ford concerning economic and community life of the street boys in Westlands.

Mama Ford buys only paper products. Other buyers in Westlands collect tin products that can bring 20 shillings per kilo. She said aluminum cans from beer, for example, are popular, and plastic products earn 3 shillings/kilo. Some boys collect only tin and steel products; others collect only paper. Steel waste can be obtained from construction sites. Mama Ford pays about 3 shillings per kilo for paper waste materials. Some boys bring to her as much as 100 kilos at a time. These boys have "stations," places where materials are available in abundance having been stockpiled by *askaris*, cleaners, and others who sell their waste products to the boys for a fee. Wamzee, discussed elsewhere, is one of those boys in our research who brings large amounts to her. One of the reasons that Wamzee's earnings and expenditures have been favorable enough to permit his movement from sleeping on the streets to having his own place is due to his ability to collect paper in large scale. Big amounts of paper products are not brought by him to Mama Ford daily, but are stockpiled for sale according to the day of the week, climatic season of the year, and the business cycle. For example, paper products are not purchased during the wet season because the paper is too heavy. Before holidays, waste products are abundant because of heavy sales in the stores. At month's end, when people are paid, there is also a lot of business and, therefore, of waste products. Mama Ford pointed out that at month's end sometimes an exceptional boy can bring in as many as 150 kilos. Bigger and therefore stronger boys dominate bulk collections and deliveries. Bigger boys, with maximal stockpiled collections, routinely do bring in as much as about 50 kilos in their bags. A common pattern is for a bigger boy to bring in 100 kilos on one day and 40 kilos on some other day the next week. Those younger boys who collect daily, such as Jacob, described in chapter 8, bring in between 10 to 15 kilos per day from such "stations" as the shopping mall, larger commercial houses, and bigger stores. Boys assign themselves to specific places based on their ability to strike a good deal with those responsible for cleaning away waste in the establishment.

Mama Ford believes that the street children are an indispensable element in the waste disposal system of Nairobi. A newspaper article in the *East African Standard* entitled "They Survive by Selling Garbage," by Othello Gruduah, agrees with her. This article states, "To a great extent, albeit insignificant and unrecognized by some in the Nairobi City Council, the scavengers are of tremendous assistance to the council, which can hardly cope with the heaps of garbage across Nairobi and its environs" (June 30, 1995: 22). The article goes on to point out that the scrap collectors, mostly street men and boys, take everything for sale to *jua kali* middlemen and women, such as Mama Ford, for eventual resale to recycling factories from "disused polyethylene bags, plastic cans, and papers, to metals and copper wires, and sell them to recycling factories" (p. 22). In 1999, an *East African Standard* article by Mildred Ngesa entitled "Huruma Residents Living in Garbage," accompanied by photographs of mounds of refuse, reported, "Although it is the business of the City Council to collect garbage, through its cleansing department, Huruma residents say they have never seen Council lorries in their estate ferrying the waste. Tired of waiting, young people in the slum want to clean up the mess, but they need tools for the job" (February 24, 1999). One of the residents is quoted as saying, "We hear, there are people who are paid to clean up the city, but we have never seen them" (p. 24).

Mama Ford has provided insightful comments gleaned from her vantage point working adjacent to a major street boy home base, Sabaima, and from her close economic ties with the street boys. She is in an ambiguous position since she herself respects and likes many of the street children and is closely linked to them economically but, at the same time, she is an outsider and is perceived as such by members of the public. On one occasion, for example, the police approached Mama Ford on foot while she and P.K. were in conversation at her weighing station. It was not clear to me precisely what they wanted from her, but as soon as he produced his research permit from the Office of the President, they smilingly walked away. It is true that Mama Ford knows a lot of secrets of interest to some outsiders such as who among the street boys might have committed a crime or who is hiding out in the community. On one occasion, for example, it came to P. K.'s knowledge that one of the street boys had killed a person elsewhere in Nairobi and had been hiding in Westlands for about one year. Mama Ford most likely knew this also. She was, for example, also deeply involved in Daniel's alleged stolen egg incident, to be discussed in the next chapter. She said that at night some of the older boys steal such things as bicycles, gas cylinders, foods, and so on. Recently, one 12-year-old street boy snatched a handbag from a woman near the International Casino not far from Sabaima and was subsequently beaten to death through mob justice.

Mama Ford emphasized that the boys do not spend a great deal of their time talking about food. In fact, some of the boys are well off enough to be choosy and can and do sometimes reject undesirable food. She said boys seen searching through dustbins are more likely to be looking for items for resale than items of food. They search dustbins, she says, primarily for valuables such as shoes, watches, key holders or anything that can be used or sold. Desperate boys, however, will search for food, especially boys who come from Koragocho and Mkuru-Reuben, two communities described in our chapter on Nairobi. A favorite food of the boys known to her is potatoes, which they cook most often by boiling mixed with cabbage and tomatoes. Bread is readily available from local bakeries and kiosks. They have a heavy starch diet, especially from the very popular fried potato chips. Far more significant to the boys, based upon her observations of their behavior and listening to their conversations, is their need for clothing and cash, the latter is by and large sufficient for a steady, if not nutritious, diet.

Mama Ford has observed that the boys beg up to about the age of 10. Between 10 and 15, they are primarily paper collectors, while those over 16 up to about 20 gradually mature into a life beyond that of a street child. A few boys she knows have become "touts" for *matatus*. Others have gone back to school. Some boys start small businesses. One boy is now shining shoes while another is selling sweets. Another boy is applying for a car wash license. A number of boys over 18 years old are now known as "transporters." They wait by the bus stage with a wagon to transport to kiosks vegetables brought to Westlands daily from up country in pickup trucks. Some boys she knows have returned home, sometimes being collected by their parents, some of whom did not know their child was on the streets. Petty criminals are among those known by Mama Ford after their lives on the streets have ended. Generally, former street boys known to her dress smartly and, for the most part, lead a "normal" life. She knows of a boy who was taken to India by an Asian man. That boy is now fully rehabilitated through education.

COMMUNITY REPRESENTED IN PHOTOGRAPHS

So as to better understand community life in Westlands as it is perceived by the boys themselves, we used a modified technique developed by researchers working among Native American Navaho in which some informants were asked to photograph those things they considered to be important in their own lives (Worth & Adair, 1970). Daniel and one other boy, on separate occasions, walked around with P. K. and indicated what scenes he should photograph to best depict what life is like for street children as perceived by them. Daniel helped us to construct a table presented here which provides places, events, and people considered most significant in the experiences of two street boys. After discussion, Daniel agreed that their choice of what to photograph would be very typical of what others would choose if asked to do so.

Table 7.1 reports what people, places and things were of importance to Daniel and the other street boy. In his and the other boys' selections, can be seen the significance of places associated with routine events in daily life. It is noteworthy that the "sociality" of the boys is indicated by the many photographic choices that contained fellow street children. A sense of sociality is, in fact, commonly observed on most occasions (with the exception of collecting waste products) when boys are seen together for activities such as bathing, eating, begging, sleeping, or in pleasurable recreational activities.

JOYS

One day "Papa" reached for a photograph held by P. K., one that showed Papa dodging among fellow "skins" in pursuit of the *mpira* (football) during a football (soccer) game held on a Sunday afternoon at a Roman Catholic church field in Westlands. The match was sponsored by the Word of Life mission and brought together 56 early-to-late teenage street boys from the Westlands area. Teams were divided into "skins and shirts," with a vigorous game heavily contested throughout. For weeks the boys told P. K. about the upcoming game with enthusiastic anticipation for the fun it would involve for the participants. It was indeed a pleasure to see the boys running and yelling excitedly about skills displayed by a good "striker" or a great save by the goalkeeper. Indeed, boys with bandaged limbs and cuts and bruises obtained from the streets merged, at least for a time, into a joyous moving mass of youth enjoying life the way many children do at some time or another in Kenya through competitive sport. Most of the boys had learned to play football in school, for some of them still a powerful memory of better days in the past. For the lucky ones, such fun might be possible again, they hoped, if a sponsor could be found for paying school fees. If only the symbolism of this athletic event could be popularized, it might combat the exclusive public symbolism of the glue bottle. This thought was in P. K.'s mind for several days after the football game was over, so intense was the positive emotional impact experienced by the boys in mpira competiton.

Not all mpira games are organized. Indeed, street children, sometimes including girls as well as boys, can be seen playing football made from rolled paper bound with thick rubber bands. Younger children can be seen playing tag and hide and seek. Boys especially, but sometimes girls, can be observed horsing around by pushing and shoving each other or by pantomiming boxing. One street boy entertained a number of street girls by showing off and pretending to be a car thief stealing a headlight while ducking out of sight of a policeman. Some street children do steal headlights, but on this occasion the sole purpose of this boy's activity was to entertain the girls. He admirably succeeded as the girls doubled up with loud laughter that, for one girl was accompanied by tears.

Street boys in Westlands play a variety of card games and also a popular game played with light and dark coffee beans or rocks thrown sequentially by opponents looking for specific color combinations known as *chaka*. Some boys play *chaka* or cards for fun, but most often such games involve gambling. In a good day, an expert *chaka* player can win several hundred shillings. Gambling with cards or betting in *chaka* is frequently seen, especially on a Sunday. One boy, for example, while relaxing at cards said, "We have nothing to do today. It is Sunday." Sundays, as other occasions for relaxation, find some boys in Westlands listening to transitor radios or watching television in a public location. Sunday bathing is a special pleasure, at such places as available boreholes or by collecting water from a friendly petrol station. Most street children do not attend church. One problem is the lack of good clothes needed to attend church. Both boys and girls enjoy putting on good clothes when they are available, and especially like nice shoes that are shined by local shoeshine men. Both girls and boys sing songs in groups; girls, for example, we observed singing while waiting for food at church distribution centers. These songs are both Christian and secular. The same girls from Jevanjee Gardens have been observed combing each other's hair or dancing while singing together. These girls also gamble while playing cards, usually small amounts such as five shillings per hand. *Chaka* is played primarily by boys.

We have described in this chapter "ritual" involvements such as funeral attendance and courtship activities that provide outlets for positive and meaningful social interactions. Even the struggle for food and coping with fears associated with police harassment provide for the children some positive experiences. For example, we have observed girls enthusiastically visit their comrades in jail, bringing along food and news of happenings on the streets. Nevertheless, Westland boys, when given money for a "treat," will often seek out *matumbo* (cow's stomach), a Kenyan delicacy, which is eaten with gusto! Eating delicacies provides pleasures even though such opportunities are rare, and street children are outside food distribution exchange at family feasts on holidays and rituals.

Survival on the streets requires a special facility with language for optimal success in coping with the intensive, often competitive social interactions among street children. There is a strong interdependence with a priority for communication skills required for success on the streets. For example, most street children know at least three languages, or four, if English is one of them. Virtually all of the street children speak an ethnic language, Kiswahili and the Kenyan youth language known as *sheng.* In Nairobi, *sheng* includes new words and word combinations drawn from Kikuyu, English, and Kiswahili. For example, the nickname Papa is the *sheng* word for "shark," or one with an abrasive personality. A good looking girl is called *kafiti* (is fit) while a child is called *katoi/mtoi* from the Kiswahili word *mtoto* (child). Many *sheng* words collected by Bryn Mawr student Caryn Groce in 1993, among street children living in Madaraka, working under the supervision of Enos Njeru, closely paralleled persons and activities experienced by them on the streets. To illustrate this finding, some examples she discovered include the following: *kakui* (to beat up); *magilogilo* (to get money); *manoka* (to be high on drugs); *masiti* (city council policeman); *mudishi* (food); *matara* (garbage), and *cabiere* (glue) (Groce, 1993).

We will discuss artistic and performance outlets enjoyed by street children in the last chapter. It should be noted here, however, that street children are becoming part of Kenyan popular cultural expressions in plays, novels, television shows, radio programs, and songs. A recent song entitled "Hoy Hoy Chokora," for example, admonishes the public to not give street children money for glue, but to give them hope instead.

Table 7.1
Self-chosen Photo Selections by Two Street Boys

Location	Content
Sabaima (home base for some boys)	Sleeping area, paper selling, paper stacks, home base
Jacaranda area (Daniel's sleeping place)	Washing clothes and body
Jacaranda area (Daniel's sleeping place)	Of himself, sitting here
Jacaranda area (Daniel's sleeping place)	A boy sleeping on cement rocks
Jacaranda area (Daniel's sleeping place)	Cooking area, his sufuria (cooking pot)
Main Westlands Island-roundabout	Sleeping area, 10 boys cooking small potatoes
Main Westlands Island-roundabout	Small boys sleeping
Riverside-wooded area outside of Westlands	Sleeping area
Riverside-wooded area outside of Westlands	Place for taking a shower
Riverside-wooded area outside of Westlands	Forest where boys hide from police
Westview-near main roundabout	Paper collection center
Westview-near main roundabout	Street girls' hangout
Oven Door Bakery, Westlands	Reduced cost chips, food from garbage handouts
Sarit Center roundabout	Place where Europeans Bring food on schedule
Street boy begging from car/pedestrians, Westlands	Work
Boys collecting paper and plastic, Westlands	Work
Boys eating from dust bin, Westlands,	Eating
Boys being given small potatoes at kiosk, Westlands	Eating
"Respected" street boy friend, Westlands	"Educated," a "friend"
Self portrait and friend, Westlands	Friendship
Two small street boys walking, Westlands	Friendship
Boys drinking alcohol, Westlands	Drinking alcohol
Boys pretending to be criminals to scare away tourists	Jesting
A sleeping boy alone, Westlands	Solitary sleeping, usual during the day
A dog	A pet

Chapter 8

Personal Profiles

Wambui, a pregnant girl of sixteen, twisted her pregnant body with seemingly athletic agility as she dodged in and out among the cars entering a crowded roundabout. While watching her cross the street, I observed drivers with strained and sometimes angry faces as they jostled for contested street space in an endless line of cars seeking to vacate the city for suburban homes. Wambui, wearing common attire for street girls, wore several layers of sweaters, and a tight-fitting dress, and was barefoot. It is unlikely that any driver noticed the glue bottle tucked tightly in her hand nor the fact that she was seven months pregnant, given that scenes of street girls dodging cars have become common in Nairobi today. Several weeks later Wambui requested that she be given a maternity dress when asked what she wanted for her assistance in taking part in a focus group session we organized for street girls. She said that running in the street or away from police was especially hazardous for a pregnant girl. In fact, Wambui had recently experienced police harassment when she was rounded up by police during a political disturbance. She was arrested, along with many other street children, all easy targets, during episodes of public lawlessness. Still later, she would be beaten by police as a criminal suspect, from which she suffered lower abdominal pains; perhaps a fact implicated in her stillborn birth. Dodging traffic is not always successful. Injury and sometimes death from traffic is not uncommon among street children. Recently street boys in Westlands said that they intended to initiate revenge against a "matatu" driver who was believed by them to have run down, perhaps intentionally, a street companion who died. The street boys think he had been thrown out of the "matatu" for not paying his fare or some other unknown reasons. The "matatu" number was marked for retaliation, but up to now nothing has come of it. (Kilbride field notes, 1996)

In this chapter our intention is to provide profiles about street boys and girls in order to testify to the complexities of their social lives as understood from the perspective of the individual person as he/she seeks to make sense out of his/her life under the most stressful of circumstances, as the previous vignette is intended to illustrate.   Still, street life is not without its pleasures and satisfactions, but always, as our profiles will show, within the context of overwhelming social circumstances that no child should ever have to endure. On the streets resilience is enhanced even in the most unfavorable of circumstances through psychological processes such as fantasy and self-identity construction so as to enhance personal self-esteem and social acceptance. Nevertheless, there is a striking degree of variation and individuality among the boys and girls that makes generalizations about them difficult. Overall, it seems best to bear in mind that generalizations would be expected to emerge in especially harsh circumstances endured by the street children on a daily basis. There are, of course, similarities in those social, economic, and cultural circumstances as background commonalties shared by the children, which are distal and proximal causes for their very presence on the streets.   Gender distinctions, for instance, are also apparent to us.   No street boy, for example, ever endures the stressful experience of moving among traffic while pregnant, as do some street girls. We attend to common experiences and perceptions among street children elsewhere in the book.   We take up here individual variation in personality, temperament, capabilities, and other factors that differentiate the children, sometimes strikingly so, among themselves.

In fact, the children themselves recognize that there are both shared circumstances and individual differences among them.   In an earlier chapter, we have reported about some of the common characteristics held by street children about themselves, which we discovered through the use of the focus group technique.   One significant cultural practice aptly reveals one way that street children recognize individual differences among themselves.   Through the use of nicknames, individual identities are constructed by means of a process of social interaction and individual labeling.   One day, without any prior knowledge of nicknaming among the street children, P. K. asked a small boy waiting near a large stack of waste products if he knew when "Josephine," the proprietor of paper, would be back from lunch. He replied that "Mama Ford" would soon return. Why had he called her that? He said that street boys use lots of nicknames, the name "Mama Ford" having been given to Josephine for her support of the opposition FORD Party, which was formed when Kenya reintroduced multiparty politics.   Mama signified an elderly and wise prestigious status in the eyes of the boys, some of whom she employed to bundle *karatasi* bought by her from other boys who collected them.   Later P. K. discovered that many street boys and girls have nicknames. The nicknames of some of the street children in our study are presented in Table 8.1.

Table 8.1
Nicknames

Nickname	Meaning
Landlord	A long-term area street boy who is also a leader in a particular location
Mrefu	A tall person who can see ahead physically and warn of imminent danger
Jothee	A slow boy in all the things he does
Wamzee	A polite, gentle boy with the characteristics of a good old man
Buda	A fat boy looking like a wealthy man. Fatness is associated with wealth
Papa	Tough like *papa* (Swahili name for shark), fights when he gets drunk, an older, long-term street boy
Madigida	A fat street girl
Mahindra	Joined the street children gounds (Westlands) when the police car Mahindra was in fashion. The term could also be a warning against arrest by the police or city council *askaris* (security personnel)
Tyson	Meaning tough girl
Maflare	A fancy-dressing girl
Cobra	An aggressive girl

The use of nicknames is a common practice found in most, if not all cultures. To think of street children having them too is one way to provide a "human" face standing behind the "lifestyles" lived on the street under the generalized category "the street child." Nicknames seem to have a way of reducing social distance as P. K. discovered when he shared his own family nickname with some of the kids. They enjoyed hearing about how when faced with the dilemma of differentiating among three generations of Philips, his great-aunt gave him the nickname "Buzzy" because he was always running around asking everyone questions. Whether or not some nicknames signify personality traits is hard to determine. Nicknames are an indication of certain social and physical distinctions observed by some in the course of shared experiences lived together on the streets. As such, nicknames serve as a good reminder that street children are individuals above all else, while at the same time sharing universally with all humans the practice of constructing nicknames to socially mark differences based on temperament, physical features, age, sex, and social backgrounds. We turn now to consider individual differences for specific street boys selected from among the Westlands' children among whom we had the best opportunity for long-term ethnographic research.

PAUL

Westlands attracts a good number of "expatriate" European and American residents in Kenya. One spot, "Gypsies," is an attractive, cozy, drinking location for those young cosmopolitans wishing an atmosphere of appeal to singles and younger couples in their twenties or thirties. Burgers and chips, for example, are available and served outside the bar, with a more formal dinning facility upstairs over the bar itself. Inside the bar a wooden floor runs from a glass-front single entrance to the "gents" and "ladies" a short distance to the rear. Along one wall are four stalls each with four wooden stools. On the other side a bar faced by 20 high stools on a crowded weekend serves many customers seated and standing, whereas the stalls provide a more intimate ambiance. Asians, Africans, and Europeans of "middle-class" standing comfortably associate at Gypsies, itself located just near an international casino and within 100 meters from a five-star hotel that caters to tourists. On the sidewalk in front of Gypsies are a small number of street boys who beg from passersby.

One day, outside of Gypsies, P. K. made himself known to a boy with yellow-stained teeth called Paul who had begged in good English from him occasionally but without success. On this day Paul had been given money by a European man pulling away from Gypsies in a large Land Rover that Paul had "watched" for him. He then came to P. K., pouted and requested bread. P. K. took him to a nearby bakery and bought Paul bread, then walked him back to Gypsies. During this walk, they saw a tall European man walking along the highway carrying his groceries home, where he lived with his Kenyan wife. "He is my friend," said Paul pointing to the familiar man P. K. had seen daily. "He gives me bread and milk." While resuming the conversation on the way back to Gypsies, a *mzungu* drove by in a car and greeted Paul by name. Paul then commented, "He helps me." It was clear after a short time that Paul was quite well connected. "Oh, yes," he responded to P. K.'s observation. "I have a lot of friends; an Asian woman gives me food." "Where do you sleep?" asked P. K., to which Paul answered that he slept in Kangemi in a house with his brother and a friend. Paul indicated that he commutes daily by bus from home, arriving in Westlands about 7:00 A.M. and returning home about 6:00 P.M. Indeed P. K. had often seen Paul waiting for an evening bus as P. K. alighted from a bus himself at the stop near his residence. Paul was usually seen wearing shoes, good ones such as a brown suede laced pair worn on the day of his first extended conversation with P.K. The street children literature makes a distinction between children "of" the street and those "on" the streets, as we pointed out in chapter 1. Paul seemed to represent a fairly "successful" style of adaptation for those who "commute" to the streets from "home," a boy "on" the streets, so that P. K. decided to follow up his first conversation with additional ones later, including a visit to Paul's home. We will next profile Paul to provide his social background to be followed by the story of Jacob, a boy "of" the streets who lives and works entirely on the streets.

Paul is 13 years old, identifies himself as a Roman Catholic (a large number in our survey are Catholic) who went to primary school and did not finish. He sometimes is "high" on glue, but not regularly, and is not often seen with a glue bottle, as this would discourage the public while begging. He uses glue occasionally to keep warm and to get courage in begging. He generally avoids locations where street boys "sleep," such as the roundabout, because the older boys would demand money from him. Paul lives with his 15 year-old brother and another boy in his teens. He said that he and his brother used to stay in Kangemi with their mother before she died over a year ago. They used to bring things home from money earned by collecting scrap metal, but the amount was so little that they begged to supplement it. Their father lives in their original home in Limuru, where Paul's two older sisters grew up and married. Their father is an alcoholic who ekes out a living on a small farm. At times, his two sons bring him money as he "cannot afford to visit Kangemi" (about 40 kilometers). They also go to Limuru to visit their grandmother, who can "give us food." Their father's present wife "chases" them away if they stay too long at their father's place. Their mother had moved away from Limuru some time back so as to earn money by selling vegetables in Kangemi. Paul estimates that he normally acquires about 100 shillings a day from begging. He can earn 50 shillings for washing cars but from a *mzungu* sometimes gets 200 shillings. He helps to park cars for "something small." Occasionally, he stays in Kangemi to collect scrap metal for sale at two shillings a kilo. All three boys help with food, rent, and charcoal-cooking requirements.

Paul's home does appear on the surface to be better than living outside on the streets. It is a small house in Kangemi, which is four by six meters, an end house near a mosquito-infested sewage swamp about 20 meters from the tarmac road. This windowless, one-roomed domicile has a wooden lockable door with a mud floor and an iron sheets roof. The wooden walls are reinforced with boxes and polyethylene papers. The 200 shillings a month rent is affordable, although the landlord has not paid for the water at the city council, so presently water is stored inside in a jerry can. Dirty clothes are hung inside the house, a place used primarily for sleeping, as it is usually late when the three boys get home after already eating out. Three latrines serve over thirty tenants in the area. The following material items were also noted in the house: two cooking *sufurias* (pots), four plates, a cooking stick, firewood, a small stool, two blankets, four bedsheets, a mattress, and a table. The boys share responsibilities and expenditures in the house for things such as soap, rent, and food. Paul said their housing problems included too few blankets, a muddy floor, little ventilation, and a lot of mosquitoes. They share with a neighbor one kerosene stove, which was taken from their mother's house after her death. Nevertheless, all in all, Paul is comfortable in his home and prefers it to sleeping on the streets.

Although Paul is "on" and not "of" the streets, he still experiences most of the stresses and strains of street life, involving as it does, begging, glue use, and generally hostile public attitudes. Paul, in fact, turned out to be a major suspect in a car theft, that occurred one night at Gypsies. P. K. had been asked by one of his former students, a current resident of Kenya, to ask the street boys if they might have some information about a car theft, which turned out to be her own car. The former student, a very perceptive observer of things Kenyan, knew that street boys near Gypsies were unlikely to be themselves car thieves, a rather more complicated criminal activity than the petty thieving usually practiced by some street children. P. K. subsequently asked one of his research assistants to inquire from Paul if he had seen or heard anything about the car theft. While talking with Paul, however, this assistant was arrested by two policemen who had come "out of the shadows," where they had been watching the street boys to catch   "accomplices" in the car theft.   The police hurriedly took the key informant to Central Police Station for investigation as the car thief. On the way to the police station, the police asked their suspect, "Why are you associating with criminals?" while describing their intent to capture the car thief.   The assistant, a youthful-looking man in his early twenties, hardly looked the part of the criminal, but it seems an extended discussion with the street children was sufficiently "suspicious behavior" to warrant his arrest. By the time P. K. learned of the arrest, to him a ludicrous episode, his assistant had, happily, been "bribed" out of the cell by one of his relatives and was back at his research work in Westlands. P. K. regretted the bribe but was told that the only alternative was a beating.

JACOB

Jacob talked comfortably into the tape recorder as he, P. K., and a veteran interviewer from a child welfare society conversed about street life in a shaded area in Westlands. The interviewer, a man well respected by street children, later commented to P. K. that their one-hour interview with Jacob was the most relaxed and informative interview in his memory. Soda and cookies had helped to contribute to the "informality" hoped for in a formal interview with prearranged questions. Perhaps all the hanging out by P. K. doing informal ethnographic interviewing had made his presence on the streets a matter of nonthreatening routine in the eyes of his informants. In fact, P. K. had spent many hours prior to the interview with Jacob, so that by the time they proceeded to the formal interviewing, Jacob was comfortable enough with P. K. to have chased other boys away from him when they begged.   Many boys never bothered begging, for they had often seen Jacob and P. K. going together to small "hotels" (food stalls) for tea, vegetables, *chapati* (fat-fried flat wheat bread) and occasionally *matumbo* (cow intestine), a special treat. Items of clothing were known to have passed from P. K. to Jacob, including pairs of shoes mentioned later. Nevertheless, in spite of reasonably good rapport, the interviewer was unable to elicit any information on drug use, stealing, or other illegal activities.   Notwithstanding, reliable autobiographical and personal material was obtained as learned through "cross-checking" techniques mentioned earlier.

After the interview, as Jacob rose to return to the streets, his 15 year-old body clearly showed signs of life lived fully on the street. Unlike Paul, Jacob is a boy "of" the streets. Cuts, bruises, and one shoe, a broken-down watch secured by a string, and a badly torn pair of trousers with a short-sleeved folded shirt were standard for Jacob. During the interview Jacob replied to a question about what caused a wound we noted he had, "I got burned with fire and nylon paper. I was warming myself by the fire; it was very cold last night. The tin I was holding had nylon paper hanging on it, which melted and dropped on me. That sore on my foot was caused by a needle that prickled me. The doctor said we should be careful of razors that we find because if cut by them we could get AIDS."

As Jacob headed back to Sabaima, his sleeping area, P. K. sadly wished he could help Jacob return to school, his constantly voiced ambition to all who would listen. One NGO had sponsored his young brother with whom he had come to the streets two years earlier after his family fled from the "tribal clashes" in Rift Valley Province. The ethnic clashes had sent many Kikuyu immigrants away from areas largely perceived to be formerly Kalenjin lands (these are some of the many Kikuyu in diaspora) driven out in what many considered to be politically motivated violence. Bows and arrows chased Jacob, two siblings, and his mother from his maternal grandmother's land. His father was no longer alive, so his mother established a small vegetables business in Kangemi from which the two boys moved into the streets in Westlands. Jacob was once in standard 4, but poverty precluded further education.

Jacob's relationship with his mother is difficult to sort out. He speaks often of his visits to Kangemi, which are rare and are only undertaken if he has about 50 shillings and some sugar to give to his mother. Repeated efforts by P. K. to meet his mother failed. Other street boys indicated that she is an alcoholic and a prostitute but definitely lives in Kangemi. Everything considered, it seems that Jacob has a fantasy life concerning his relations with his mother. She could not be visited by us on a number of abortive occasions without Jacob first having a bath, a haircut, and new clothes. These were ideals that Jacob could not live up to, and he seemed to be projecting these ideals to his mother as well. In time P. K. did not press the issue of Jacob's mother for fear that his fantasies, should they exist, would be consciously and perhaps painfully confronted by him. Clearly, however, his "identity construction" seemed to require a positive maternal figure, one that P. K. never saw.

Jacob's home is located in an area bounded on four sides in turn by kiosks, clothing stalls, a wall, and a fenced side street with the entrance to the sleeping area beside the clothing stalls. In this roughly 30 by 60 meters area, as many as 30 street boys sleep on cardboard and nylon paper beds on several raised granite stone slabs; they huddle around fires near the stones, sleeping together in clusters of small groups. About a dozen to 15 boys like Jacob sleep in Sabaima almost nightly, while others are infrequent residents, depending on the day of the week. On certain days, for example, food is distributed by a church group, and boys come to Westlands for this reason while others change locations to avoid the police, and so on. No girls reside at Sabaima, although some do visit their boyfriends there. The buildings surrounding Sabaima afford some protection from the cold winds. Two boreholes provide water, and several large trees offer shade while a convenient place for defecation is available in the bushes astride the trees. Bhangi is available in these bushes and is rolled and smoked with waste papers.

We saw in an earlier chapter how an "authority" hierarchy exists among street boys based on age. In the local social organization, Jacob is not a leader but seems to get along well with most of his colleagues. His age positions him between the older and the younger boys. One boy commented that Jacob's moods are affected when he is on glue. He is usually low-key ("slow and deliberate") in his disposition. When on glue, however, he abruptly changes, seeming overly hostile to others.

Sabaima offers an excellent working condition for some of the boys sleeping there. Earlier we described the work of Mama Ford, whose paper collection business is in Sabaima. Jacob is a regular paper collector and has a close working relationship with Mama Ford. Rainy times are, however, difficult for both of them, as she cannot purchase wet papers from him. During slow times, such as when it rains or when the recycling plants close for repairs, Jacob earns money by begging and by parking cars.

Jacob never seems to have fun as compared to most of the boys. He displayed mood swings throughout P. K.'s relationship with him, which began with a clearly understood statement that he could not sponsor him in school but would help out with food and clothes. Jacob understood that P. K. was a *mwalimu* (teacher) and was therefore not wealthy but needed Jacob's assistance in writing a book in which street boys could speak out about themselves. For this reason, it seemed unlikely to P. K. that he was a primary source for Jacob's mood swings. At times, in fact, "friendship" between Jacob and P. K. seemed an appropriate word while at other times "avoidance" and sullenness were evident. Such moods seemed rare in other boys. As time went on, it became clear that glue addiction was taking more visible hold on Jacob than was evident in the early days of his association with us. Overall, Jacob's world contained more than enough stressful components such that on those occasions when he was at ease, for example, when wearing a gift or enjoying a meal with P. K., there seemed to be solace for Jacob in small things shared in friendship.

Jacob described his own typical day, verified by observation, as beginning with prayers of thanksgiving. He is a Catholic who rarely goes to church, as attendance in his view requires clean clothes and a bath with costly soap. He used to enjoy Sunday school back in Rift Valley Province. If he has money, after a breakfast of hot maize porridge or tea and bread, he sets out to collect waste paper. On Fridays and Sundays he does not collect papers because buyers have no money to purchase them from him. These are days for resting from waste paper collection. Jacob is not attuned to clock time or the idea of three meals a day. Instead, when he feels hungry he goes to look for money by begging, for example. If he gets money, he goes to eat. For recreation, Jacob watches television outside the Asian shops or listens to the radio if one of the boys has one. He is rarely seen in groups of boys playing card games or otherwise enjoying themselves. Jacob enjoys mostly bathing and then sitting and talking to other boys. He has infrequently played football with fellow street children who use a ball made from rolled papers tied with strings. Jacob claims to have no girlfriends, especially since he is aware of AIDS through unprotected sex. Jacob has been arrested once for "loitering," which is ironic given that he lives primarily to work, assisted at times by sniffing glue and by strong fantasies of an idealized previous family and school life.

MAINA

Maina's circumstance is typical of a child born in a large urban family headed by a single parent and facing severe economic deprivation. He is featured in this case study to illustrate how a hostile and impoverished social and physical environment can adversely affect the social, emotional, and cognitive development as well as the health and physical growth of a youngster in middle childhood. It is precisely such a domestic environment that is frequently a "push" factor toward some children to become children "on" the streets. Maina was interviewed by C. S.

Maina is 12 years old and the ninth child in a family of ten. He has seven sisters and two brothers, aged between 8 and 30 years. He is in standard five in an informal school located about one kilometer from his mother's house. He is the only child in the family who is attending school, since his younger sister (age 8) is not yet in school, and all his older brothers and sisters dropped out of school primarily because of the lack of fees or pregnancy.

Maina is too small for his age but over age for his class at school. He could easily pass for nine years old. He looks malnourished and has rashes on his face and arms. He is withdrawn but aggressive when he plays with his friends in school and at home. He usually chases them away whenever they try to take his wooden toy guns that he makes himself. His school attendance is irregular, partly because of illness, lack of school fees, uniform, and books. His academic performance is far below average, primarily because of poor attendance. He speaks good Kiswahili (a national language in Kenya), fluent Kikuyu (his vernacular), but very little and broken English. His teachers say he has a problem with reading and writing. He shows little interest in school and his homework.

Maina's mother is 45 years old, divorced, and the head of her own household. She has no education. She was married for only six years to a carpenter and, among her eight children, she had three children with him and had the rest (including Maina) with other men whom she could not marry because they were already married. Maina does not know his own father. The mother came to Nairobi with her former husband from Muranga District 25 years ago to seek wage employment. They could not find a job and divorced soon after. She cited cruelty and drunkenness as the major causes of their divorce. She said she was constantly battered. She also said the ex-husband was irresponsible and could not provide for her and their three children. After divorce, she changed residence several times because of nonpayment of rent and finally built one small room measuring about 10 by 10 feet in one of the city slums. The house is poorly ventilated, made of mud walls and an iron roof. It has no electricity and running water, but she owns the plot where she lives.

C. S. found out that there are 12 people who live and eat in this one room. They include Maina's mother, six of her children, and five grandchildren. Five of her seven daughters stay with her in the same household, and each of them has a child, although none of them are married. Some of her grandchildren work on the streets as parking boys but sleep at home. Two of her daughters, who are also unmarried and have children, stay with her in the same housing estate and mainly depend on her for support. The daughters are unemployed.

Maina's mother is a hawker. She buys and sells fruits and vegetables in an open-air market within the slum area. She has no land or relatives in the rural areas and has no plans to ever go back there. She has only one brother in the rural areas; they rarely exchange visits and hardly interact. When she is away in the market, her older daughters usually care for their younger siblings. One of her older sons, who also lives with her in the same household, works as a *matatu* tout in town. He would like Maina to quit school and become a tout like himself. Only the mother and her older son contribute income to the family, but their earnings are too meager to provide for the basic necessities of life such as food, clothing, water, and health care. She says she has problems paying school fees and buying schoolbooks for Maina. According to her, the books are too expensive. The school fees for Maina are 100 Ksh. (U.S. $1.60) per month. No other member of the family is employed. Sometimes when the family has completely run out of food, they go to a local church organization for free food and other gifts like used clothing. The resources of the organization are, however, dwindling because of heavy demand from the needy. When the children are sick, she usually takes them to the nearest health clinic, which is about four kilometers away. She identified malaria, pneumonia, and diarrhea as some of the most common diseases afflicting the family.

Maina's approach to work is remarkable. He is hardworking and plays multiple roles at home. Occasionally he helps his mother to sell vegetables in the nearby open-air market although it was reported that sometimes he keeps part of the proceeds to buy cigarettes without his mother's knowledge. His mother disapproves of his smoking habits and occasionally reprimands him. He also sells old newspapers and cans, works as a parking boy, and washes cars in the company of some street boys who are his friends. He engages in such activities mainly after school and on weekends to get an independent income, as he puts it. Sometimes he skips school to go to work. It was not possible for C. S. to establish what exactly he does with the money, but he claims he gives his mother part of the income, although she denied it. On more than one occasion, he had been found with a half-full packet of cigarettes and a plastic bottle containing glue. He is believed to be smoking and sniffing glue. His elder brothers are heavy smokers and also drink quite a bit. Maina has been found fighting other boys in school on several occasions, and each time the teacher punished them. One day they started fighting as they were walking home. This time they were seen by an *askari* patrolling the area and were picked up, warned, and released the same day.

Despite the negative forces against him, Maina is constantly trying, through his own agency, to adapt to an increasingly challenging environment with limited social and economic opportunities. He has adopted certain coping mechanisms, his "survival strategy," because he does not seem to see much future in his education and does not receive or expect much support from his family and the community. He experiences a difficult home life and attempts to cope with this by getting away from his family to go out in search of adventure. He oscillates between home, school, and the street. This lifestyle inevitably gets him into a lot of trouble with his peers, mother, teachers, and law enforcement agencies, but it also does represent a personal drive toward autonomy and greater self-management capability. He is trying to get a handle on his life and in the process violates some cultural rules and values and drifts into what is broadly perceived as antisocial behavior.

DANIEL

Daniel and P. K. sat together in the Pizza Garden, their eyes glancing at a large TV set carrying a European football match while they waited for their drinks and pizza. Around their table sat late afternoon patrons, some alone at the bar, others in groups at tables drinking and conversing while listening to a live band, viewing TV or simply observing people. Daniel blended nicely into the informally dressed Saturday evening crowd of young men and women relaxing after shopping or before heading out elsewhere for home, a house party, or a nightclub. Some men wore suits and tie. Daniel was not out of place dressed in a pair of slacks, a short-sleeved sport shirt, windbreaker coat, and locally made leather Bata shoes.

Daniel looked big and muscular for his 18 years. Few would have guessed that he was a street boy who slept regularly nearby in a fenced, rocky space, interspersed with bushes and grassy spots. Earlier in the day, Daniel and P. K. had photographed his bushy living space that afforded him some privacy, protection from wind, and a good place for defecation. A petrol station at one corner of his "home" was a good source of water for washing and cooking, often using discarded food given to him at local restaurants.   Large rocks afforded him a hidden place to store his *sufurias* (cooking pots) and blanket during the day.

Daniel and P. K., while watching television, discussed the previous night's census data that he and another street boy would continue to collect for an entire week.   Daniel very much liked an opportunity to work for pay as our research assistant.   It also provided him an opportunity to try to manipulate P. K. for additional gifts and to exercise leadership and to be seen in the company of a novelty represented by a resident anthropologist.   P. K. had originally been drawn to Daniel by his extroverted, charming personality, which, judging by the esteem that he enjoyed among most of his peers, could be said to be charismatic. He smiled easily, often with a keen sense of his social situation, which required strategic social interactions for survival on the streets.   He easily understood our research objectives and saw in P. K. someone to be manipulated while at the same time, profiting himself by enhancing our objectives.

At the same time Daniel worked hard at what Erving Goffman (1982) once called 'Face Work' to maintain a positive identity in his community, one that enabled him to imagine a future world that would see him one day off of the street gainfully employed, perhaps as a truck driver or taxi operator.   His identity talk (Snow and Anderson 1993) regularly portrayed himself as a victim of circumstances whereas some people who knew him over the years began increasingly to see Daniel as a "con" man, in the precise words of one woman who knows him well.   Daniel's life story strongly reveals not only his own sense of initially being "led" by others into a life on the streets that included alleged crime but also represents common patterns of street entry and survival experienced by many other street boys.   We consider now Daniel's life story. He provided information about his life in one lengthy interview and on other occasions during informal discussions.

Daniel's Life Story

Daniel began his life story interview at age 14 by describing his favorable life at that time in a boarding school in western Kenya that changed when his father died in 1989, and Daniel could no longer raise his school fees beyond standard 8. He continued,

After the burial I started seeing that my life started to be hard. After a while, my mother told me that after struggling to look for money, she could not get any. So, she told me that I was free to do what I think is best for me. Without wasting time I told my mum I would sell some of our chickens to get money to take me to Nairobi. After selling chickens, I set out by bus for Nairobi, where I intended to look for work. When I started my journey one day very early in the morning, I had 400 shillings (then about 10 dollars). Remember, I had never before been to Nairobi or traveled alone! When the bus stopped in Nakuru, I decided to leave the bus station and have a look around the town. I saw very interesting things at the town market that impressed me so much the bus left without me! Later, I looked for a place to sleep before nightfall, but after some hours I decided to sleep on a street corridor. That was the time I realized that I am really alone! I dreamt badly that night and was awakened early in the morning by police asking me, "Where are you staying? Who are you with?" I answered that I was from western Kenya and was alone. The police advised me to go to the police station, where I would be helped, but instead I was beaten badly throughout the next night. Later I was taken to court where the magistrate ruled that I should be taken to the children's remand.

In the remand where I stayed for over a year, I first met my close friend called Wakidongo, who later suggested to me that we run away together. My friend told me he would jump from the place first and as he did so, I followed him, and we ran together to the forest. We ran until we could hear no sound. After asking if I was all right, Wakidongo said we needed to get rid of our remand uniforms. At my suggestion we discarded our outer remand shirts and continued on our journey. Unfortunately, my friend had never been to school and did not know east from west. Fortunately, my watch had a compass so we headed towards Nairobi. Later we reached Kangemi (in Nairobi), where we joined some street children and got clothes from them. My street life now started! Wakidongo brought me to another place in Nairobi called South B, where we started surviving. After about a year my friend ran away, but I had already made lots of new friends, including another good friend called Shoti, from Tanzania. He led me to another part of the city called Eastleigh Estate where we survived together. When I informed Shoti that I wanted to go home to western Kenya, he suggested we could get money by stealing a radio cassette worth 6,000 shillings. We sold that cassette for 4,000 shillings, after which we ran away, and I followed Shoti here to Westlands where I have survived for several years. My life here has been good simply because of the help I have received from a priest and an American woman who helps the children here. Also, I have worked hard in collecting papers.

While watching the international football match mentioned above, Daniel explained how he used to enjoy playing football while in school. He also said he enjoyed the company of girls and still does. After the football match ended, P. K. ordered another round of drinks, and we continued our conversation.

Jail

Daniel explained that his term to survive refers to a variety of means needed for survival on the streets. He has, for example, begged, collected papers for sale, been involved in petty thefts, worked as an *askari* (watchman), and most recently earned money as a superb research assistant. He added that he had been in and out of jail, always in his own well-argued view for mistaken reasons. In jail, Daniel has been toughened up such that life on the streets seems mild by comparison. Concerning his life in jail, Daniel gave the following account:

In remand I found that everything was hard. I found that it is "another world." I found in jail everything is different; we were taken as slaves. For food, we were given porridge in the morning. At 1:00 P.M. we took our lunch, only given a piece of *ugali* (corn meal) and a glass of salty water. At 8:00 P.M. we were given our supper, a small spoon of beans and *ugali*. Where we were sleeping, in the rooms we found some blankets. Those blankets are the ones some people who had AIDS were sleeping on. When they died, we were the ones who were going to sleep on them. When we slept on them, I found that the blankets were full of lice, so I decided I was not going to sleep on those blankets. I decided instead to sleep in the toilet. I slept in the toilet for one week until I decided to just return and sleep on those blankets. I stayed in remand for two and half months; then I went to court. By good luck I presented a good case and was released.

Mkosti—A Victim of HIV—Daniel's Sympathetic Story

Daniel has seen many tough luck stories in his short life. In spite of his own problems, Daniel never seemed to be depressed or down on his luck. No matter how bad things got for him, there were always many friends and acquaintances for whom he showed genuine sympathy. He has helped, for example, to arrange funerals for street children friends who have died of AIDS, violence or car accidents. One girl whom he felt very badly about, who eventually died of AIDS, was Mkosti, whom he described as follows before her death.

Mkosti was 15 years old. She came on the streets when she was only 10 years old. Mkosti schooled up to standard 5. She stopped schooling after her father passed away. Since her father passed away, she came on the streets begging for money. She has been begging money for the last three years. She also got money from sex, for example. She told me that one evening an Arabian guy came with a car and called her. When she went closer to the car, she was asked if she would feel happy if he buys her dinner. So she entered in the car. The Arabian guy took Mkosti to his home, whereby Mkosti could not discover where she was. She was welcomed in the home, then she was told to go and have a shower. The guy told her not to worry and to feel free. After playing sex, she went and took a shower again and came from the bathroom wearing new clothes. She was given food, a delicious dinner, then they went to sleep. The following morning, she was given 6,000 shillings. She went on with her normal life on the streets. After some months she started feeling sick all over her body. She was taken to the hospital. The doctor told her that she had to be admitted. After four days we went back to Kenyatta Hospital, and we were told that Mkosti was suffering from HIV. Since then she has been sleeping on the streets of Ngara. Her street girlfriends and we boys sometimes feed her. She normally says that she is waiting for her death. She is suffering too much. She is thin and she rarely eats. I pray God to help Mkosti to live many days with us.

When their pizza was finished, Daniel walked P. K. back to his residence, after which he left to return early next morning with his census counts of those areas where street boys regularly sleep at night in Westlands.

A significant reason that Daniel is able to sustain a positive self-image needed to carry on his "survival" strategies in very difficult circumstances is that he is able to maintain a largely conventional self-identity. He sees himself as a person who comes from a very good family, had some fine education, and possesses the means needed to survive on the streets made necessary mainly by bad circumstances resulting from his father's death. He remains eager to find a sponsor to help him leave the streets by getting more qualifications for a paying job. In his view there is "nobody wise on the streets." Though Daniel has been accused of stealing, for example, and has spent time in jail, it is not his own morals or personality that is at issue. Rather, unfortunate circumstances have, he insists, conspired on occasion to trap him as one who seems unjustifiably to others to be a petty criminal. Daniel's identity negotiations with everybody with whom he interacts regularly can be illustrated by what became for P. K. "the egg incident."

Over several years, Daniel and P. K. rehearsed at his prompting whether or not Daniel "really stole the eggs." Most people on the street said he had. The incident at issue concerning the "stolen eggs" occurred one summer just after P. K. returned to Bryn Mawr College to teach. At this time, Daniel was arrested, allegedly for stealing eggs. His arrest was frustrating to P. K. because he had left behind for him 9,000 shillings so Daniel could take lessons for a driver's license according to his wishes to become a driver. After Daniel spent some months in jail, and according to our contacts with no end in sight, P. K. reluctantly released his money to enable one of our other research assistants (not a street boy) to go to school for his driving license.

By the following summer, Daniel had just been released from jail and enthusiastically resumed his research work with us. The consensus on the streets was still that "Daniel probably stole the eggs." Nevertheless, to this day Daniel still denies that he did so. Perhaps he believed that the support of his employer, P. K., and his church patron (to whom he also expressed his innocence and who subsequently sponsored his driving lessons) might be in jeopardy if he was "really" a thief. Certainly, Daniel's identity talk is very convincing in regard to his innocence about the egg incident, told with conviction by one who intensely believes in what he is saying. This is what Daniel said about the egg incident.

Daniel's Egg Story

It was Monday morning when I had bad luck. Where I was living the businessmen knew me very well. On this day one of my friends with whom I sleep together at night by the name of Saidi Juma stole 24 crates of eggs and brought them to our sleeping place. When I woke up in the morning, I saw some businessmen from nearby looking at me. After a while they said, "Daniel is staying with a bad group, so he must know the person who stole the eggs." They commanded me to "tell us who stole the eggs." I answered that I did not know anything. One of the men said we are going to beat you until you tell us who stole the eggs. They started beating me with sticks and stones. I thought they were going to kill me. They were beating me so much! It is acceptable to administer "mob justice" here in Kenya. I agreed that I knew the person who stole the eggs and then asked them to take me to the police station. By my good luck the owner of the eggs agreed with me, so I was taken to the police station. At the police station I was taken to the cells, and the egg owner wrote up his statement about the stolen eggs. I stayed for five days at the police station, and then I was taken to court and later to the magistrate. I pleaded innocent to stealing the eggs, and I was then taken back to my cell. While in the cell I was told by some prisoners that my case was very easy compared to their own. One man taught me how to argue my case. He asked for 100 shillings to teach me and I gave him the 80 that I had in my pocket. He told me to look for a paper and a pen, after which I wrote everything down about how to argue my case. Later the charges were eventually dropped and I was released, but I still successfully argued my case to the judge according to my innocence.

We were subsequently told that the egg owner in fact dropped the charges when a benefactor reimbursed him for his stolen eggs. Daniel was then released from jail. The egg incident illustrates that Daniel, like most street children, is regularly involved in a frequently ambiguous process of negotiated identity, one that is made all the more ambiguous by the marginal and stigmatized social status of the street child.

MARGARET

Our research assistant, Michael, went back to bring us more bread to go with our beef stew as Margaret and P. K. continued their conversation over lunch. The three of them had a meal in a crowded small restaurant located not far from Jevanjee Gardens across from the street area where Margaret slept each night with other street girls she considered her friends, although she feared some of them stole her things on occasion. Margaret reminded P. K. a lot of Daniel. She is a person who smiles easily and finds conversation to be joyous. When among her female peers, she speaks openly about many subjects concerning their community life described earlier. Today was no exception with us. She was dressed in a colorful sweater on top of the *kitenge* cloth wrapped around her legs, waist, and shoulders. She was barefoot. While they ate, she freely described how she got the scar on her cheek and a recent cut on her leg, which was bandaged. Her body clearly showed the effects of the violence that sometimes inflicted itself on her. The scar and the cut were incurred while resisting the unwelcome advances of street boys during the night. For this reason Margaret preferred sleeping with other girls under the watchful eyes of an older boy who, for a fee, protected them during the night from street boys who might rape or steal from them. Like many other girls she slept on cardboard on the ground with her friends in an enclosed area behind a building across from Jevanjee Gardens, a good place for begging during the day. We had spent time with Margaret in the days before the lunch interview, for example, going with her for breakfast of hot porridge and tea as well as conversations around her home base of Jevanjee Gardens. Not once, however, did she directly reveal to us that she engaged in "survival sex," although she told us a lot about it. Some street boys considered her to be involved, but given that prostitution is a "stigmatized" practice, it seemed that Margaret's own sense of dignity and self-identity clearly did not make such conversation with us a priority. About her friends who do engage in prostitution, she reported the following to my research assistant.

The street boys have several ways of making money, for example, starting small businesses and looking for waste papers to take for weighing and to get money as a result. The girls claim that the street boys are able to survive because they have strength to do many things including stealing (theft). We girls only get money through begging, and we sometimes go without eating, if we are denied money by the public. Moreover, the young girls sometimes go without eating for begging is their only consistent source of income. The older street girls are somehow lucky when it reaches night because some of them turn out to be prostitutes in bars while others go to nightclubs to make money and others are taken by very rich people to satisfy their sexual desires. These rich people come for the street girls as late as midnight in expensive cars, for they fear being identified by other people. Most of them are businessmen and a mixture of blacks, Asians and whites. The majority of these men go to street girls with the dangerous motive of infecting them with sexually transmitted diseases, then they are abandoned and left to suffer, yet they are sometimes given a lot of money after that.

We can see from Margaret's account that prostitution is embedded in the context of their limited opportunities to get money. Street girls, who overall do regularly practice prostitution, do not generally think of themselves as "prostitutes," but rather they, by and large, see prostitution as an opportunity to make money when the occasion arises. Overall, they do not self-identify as prostitutes; nor do most members of the public consider them primarily as such. Rather they are "street girls," a negative and "master" label. Margaret very much, for example, self-identifies as a mother, a subject of regular conversation in her life.

At our lunch interview, Margaret filled us in on the major events in her life. She is 19 years old and the mother of a one-and-a-half-year-old son. The father of her child was a "pickpocket" before he died in a drowning accident while bathing in their home area of Kayole in the Eastlands of Nairobi. They had fallen in love and then "started pushing" (having sex) after meeting in town. She does not know any of his relatives. After his death, she moved to Jevanjee Gardens. Her son is cared for by Rescue Dada, an NGO that specifically serves street girls, especially those with babies. She described her life as a street girl as follows, "After dropping out of primary school, I met some girls on the streets who taught me how to ask for money, and if I refused to do so, they beat me up until I got used to pleading for money. Nowadays, I beg along the streets, in shops, and even marketplaces and the little I get, I give to my son."

When her son is not at Rescue Dada, she takes him along when she begs. Concerning her parents, Margaret said that her mother drinks a lot of alcohol and does not care about her. When she goes home to Nakuru for a visit, she looks for rotten food in the rubbish pit to eat. Her mother has no idea where she is now. Her father died a long time ago. She relies on her fellow street girls,

Catholic nuns, Rescue Dada, and her own skills for survival. Margaret lives entirely outside of family connections, either consanguineal or affinal. When faced with major problems, such as a failure to get money from begging or when her son is sick and there is no money for medicine, she says, "I pray so that God helps."

The following summer, after our initial summer's research, we were able to have a follow-up interview with Margaret. She had, in the meantime, given birth to a baby girl. She no longer sleeps across from Jevanjee Gardens because the area was fenced off since street boys, she said, used to hide stolen goods there. Nowadays, her former sleeping companions are scattered along streets far from Jevanjee Gardens. She had visited her two children at Rescue Dada several days before our meeting with her. Margaret's oldest child was taken recently by Rescue Dada to the hospital for treatment of pneumonia. She said that at Rescue Dada, "[her] children are more healthy than when they are with [her] on the streets because there they are given food, they sleep well, and are given medicine when sick. On the streets the children are often cold and without food." She has grown close to the youngest child in the first year of her life. Her younger child, a girl named Agnes after Margaret's mother, provides Margaret with a chance to "keep my mother's name alive by transferring it to my daughter." This attitude is, of course, consistent with our view that some street girls desire to have children for cultural reasons, an attitude derived from generally pronatalist norms as reinforced by Kenyan indigenous beliefs and indigenous institutions. She still does not know the father of her daughter and, as we have noted previously, her son's father was killed in an accident. She therefore gets no assistance from the fathers of her children. She visited her grandmother eight months ago, and Margaret said, "I know she is missing me as much as I am missing her." Margaret's positive feelings about her family suggest that although girls overall seem to maintain more infrequent home visits than boys, such familial relationships are not by any means absent and may also be "in the heart" even though face-to-face encounters are minimal.

In May 1999, we were able to locate Margaret to catch up on events in her life. She was pregnant again, four months, and did not know the father's identity. She was good-spirited and very happy to see us, although she looked tired and old beyond her years. Her two previous children were now in a children's home outside of Nairobi. Margaret requested another maternity dress from us, which we gave her in addition to food and other clothing. We discussed news of other girls known to us and the nickname we wanted to use for her in our book, which she approved. Through Margaret, we were able to contact Wanjiru.

On her interactions with street girls in general, the girls move frequently as do boys. Of the girls known to us, none of them live in the specific locations they did three years ago, when we first met them. Nevertheless, some of them occupied sleeping spaces on what might be called a "greater Jevanjee Garden" territory and were thus able to trace each other or came into contact from time to time. Margaret confirmed our conclusion that opportunities to leave the streets were very limited for girls. She mentioned getting married, employment as a housemaid, hairdresser, or prostitute among those known to her. Another street girl, Angel, known to us, had been imprisioned and was now married to a driver and living in Kayole.

WANJIRU

Daniel and Wanjiru came together for a meeting with P. K. We had asked Daniel to help us to meet some street girls since they were rarely seen in our research in Westlands. Daniel explained that girls sometimes came to Westlands for begging, and recently on Wednesdays, when food was given out by a charitable program sponsored by an American. According to Daniel, the boys had chased the girls away to better control access to begging resources in Westlands. Nevertheless, some romantic ties still existed between the girls, who resettled in Jevanjee Gardens and elsewhere, and some boys still living in Westlands. Wanjiru, for example, was still 'pushing' a boy in Westlands known as Wamzee. For our interview, Wanjiru, Daniel, and P. K. sat on the grass near the main roundabout in Westlands. Wanjiru, 24 years old, was extroverted, with a good facility for conversation, which we had in English and Kiswahili. She was in her early twenties and wore a cotton dress with a sweater. Her head was covered with a scarf, and her shoes were torn. Wanjiru explained that she had completed standard 5. She left home because of poverty. Her father died when she was still young. Presently her mother lives in Mathare Valley, where she sells vegetables. When she left school because of a lack of school fees, she met some girls who convinced her to leave school for good and take up street life. She met a man who made her pregnant. They decided to take up residence in Korogocho, constructing a house made from cartons. She continued to tell us that the police used to come and beat them, as her husband was involved in some illegal activities. She eventually left him after he "moved" with other women and was also jailed. She said, "For these reasons I started a new life." In 1996, she slept near the Uchumi store near Jevanjee Gardens. She described a typical activity as follows, "In the morning I wake up and go to city market next to Uchumi. When I go there, I find things like potatoes, bananas, and tomatoes. After that I look for a big tin, some pieces of paper, matches and do my cooking. When I need salt, I go to where they sell chips and I am given." Wanjiru begs in addition to scavenging for food in the market area.

The following year after our first interview, we reestablished contact with Wanjiru to assist in finding street girls who were pregnant as part of our effort to learn about pregnancy among street girls. She was helpful to us and revealed more information about herself as well. Wanjiru, for instance, in addition to her first child, now seven years old, also has a three-year-old boy. The boy's father is a street boy. He used to help with food prior to his arrest. She said, "I am no longer smoking cigarettes and *bhangi* (marijuana) and have left sniffing glue. I don't also fall in love with whomever I meet as I used to before. I just realized that all these men just cause me to waste a lot of money." According to Daniel, Wanjiru on occasion made good money at survival sex. One *mzungu,* he said, gave her several thousand shillings for sex. As in conversation with other street girls, survival sex never directly came up with Wanjiru, suggesting that this is, at least in some cases, not a central part of their identity.

Daniel and P. K. were able to interview Wanjiru's seven-year-old son, Eric. His own mood reflected his mother's hope of finding an educational sponsor for her child, but with a realistic feeling that doing so is not likely. Eric, named after Wanjiru's father, told us sadly, "I would like to go to school, but money is not available. I used to feel ashamed by begging for money, but I was forced by my mother. I ask myself what kind of a mistake I did or my mother did to God." Wanjiru confides that "when I think about Eric, I feel like running crazy. I never get an answer when thinking about how I can leave the streets." In 1998, Wanjiru's younger son died of cerebral malaria; she was hoping to raise money for his burial costs.

Margaret sent word to Wanjiru so that we were able to interview her in May 1999. She was temporarily living in Mathare Valley in the house of her mother, who was in the hospital. She planned to return to the streets when her mother was better. Our female research assistant, who had interviewed both Margaret and Wanjiru in Kikuyu, agreed with P. K. that both girls are very intelligent and possessed an impressive social presence. Wanjiru expressed a desire to go to a rural village if she could find someone there to marry her, an idea that was not especially appealing to Margaret. Wanjiru was tired of the survival sex, which she practices, and the hard city life she lives. She gave more information to us on her past and other girls' use of contraception, including "the pill" and "injections." Wanjiru hoped to get a coil fitted in the future, as she is currently practicing survival sex. She said men come in cars and collect girls from the streets and go to lodges or to homes where *askaris* are paid to look the other way. Many men will trick them and pay nothing, but she requests 500 shillings. Both Wanjiru and Margaret expressed a fear of AIDS and said they were frequently requested to perform nonconventional sex by men from various ethnic groups and nationalities, sometimes with a threat of a gun if refused.

VERONICA

Wanjiru introduced Veronica to us. Veronica was seven months pregnant and had agreed to help us in our attempt to document social circumstances surrounding pregnancy in the lives of pregnant street girls. P. K. and his assistant, Michael, interviewed Veronica. In our interview, she was quite cooperative but not expansive in her discussion with us. Veronica seemed on the whole to be stoic in temperament, not surprising given her circumstance at the time of our meeting. On occasion we had observed her taking glue and lying about Jevanjee Gardens with a depressed appearance. Tragically, her baby was dead at birth, perhaps as a result of severe kicks she had suffered from the police. Veronica, like Margaret and Wanjiru, is a Kikuyu and speaks her ethnic language and also Kiswahili. She left school after standard 4.

In response to our specific questions, she revealed the following facts about her pregnancy. She said, "Street boys don't beat you if they know that you are pregnant; some boys and girls will give food if they have money." She continued, "I don't have much sickness, but sometimes during the day I do suffer from slight headache. I long to eat rice, beans, bananas, and passion fruits, but rarely have money to do so. I get all my money from begging. I never dream about having a baby or my pregnancy. I stopped having sex in the third month."

Veronica, age 17, reported that she still has contact with the 20-year-old street boy who impregnated her. Unlike many girls who said their partner would run away when faced with a pregnant girlfriend, Veronica's boyfriend said he would help out. She has gone with him for four years. Though in 1996 she lived at Jevanjee Gardens, she met her boyfriend in Korogocho, where she used to live with her parents. They don't know her present whereabouts. She had been sent to an approved school (reform) because she had refused to go to regular school. She ran away from the approved school. When asked to describe her economic life from the time she left school, Veronica said, "I started to sell charcoal and went to live in Dandora Estate, where I met some girls who convinced me to take a bus to town with them. Once here, we saw people asking for money, so we then also started to ask for money from people." Veronica pointed out to us that she is now staying either at the same place with her boyfriend or on the streets. Unlike many mothers whom she has seen or heard about who have aborted their babies, she will never throw away her baby "even if he is disturbing me" (see Kilbride, 1990, for a discussion of infanticide in Kenya).

A year after Veronica's pregnancy in 1997, we caught up with her along Kenyatta Avenue, where she sleeps. Veronica was wearing a blouse and *kitenge* skirt under a green zip-up jacket. She wore brown-laced red shoes, a hat, and had sparkles on her face remaining from the nightclub where she had been the previous evening. She left behind her fellow street girls, who had been grooming her hair, and came with us for a luncheon interview. She had moved from Jevanjee Gardens and now slept with seven girls and three boys on Kenyatta Avenue.

Veronica said her baby died after several weeks on the streets because of exposure to the cold and malaria. She had no money for burial so the hospital buried her baby for her at their hospital. The father of her dead baby was now in jail for three months for stealing from hawkers. She plans to wait for his release so as to continue their relationship since he had helped out before. The maternity dress that we had given to her the previous year was still in her possession at her mother's home in Korogocho. She will use the dress again if she becomes pregnant. She said girls visit their homes like boys but have fewer opportunities to get money for their parents through stealing, collecting *karatasi,* washing cars, and even begging. She can trust girls far more than boys, whom she considers to be duplicitous.

Veronica no longer associates much with the girls of Jevanjee Gardens since they were dispersed when a restaurant was built there. She still sees some of them, however, from time to time when she sleeps at City Market. Her present companions beg near the Casino movie theater. She continues to go, however, to the Anglican Church for food and for bathing. She knows many girls who practice survival sex, but they mostly live elsewhere, such as along River Road. She has been picked up in cars by men to be taken to a nightclub. Once when refusing sex she was dumped along the highway far from town by a wealthy African man.

Veronica no longer feels so bad about losing her baby because caring for it was very difficult. In fact, she doesn't want more children while alone. Veronica is not alone in recognizing the demands that childcare can impose on the life of a single street girl. One informant, for example, a teenage street girl, said she was happy she didn't have a baby, as that would put her in a tight situation. She said, "Feeding a baby is another hell." Thus, it is clear that while some girls see having a baby as a strategic advantage in begging or eliciting group assistance, others clearly do not. In 1999, we were told by Margaret and Wanjiru that Veronica was now married to the father of her child, a former street boy, and together they have a carton-and-polyethylene house in the slums of Kayole.

GENDER

Based on our long-term work with boys and our research one summer with subsequent follow-up interviews with girls like Margaret, Wanjiru, and Veronica, it is our impression that occupational flexibility is less available to girls than it is to boys. For example, none of the street girls known to us were observed to be involved in waste paper collection or even casual labor such as employment as an *askari* (guard) of various properties during nighttime. Their only recourse to money appears to be survival sex and begging. Opportunities for income after a girl leaves the streets are also limited, as we have seen. Boys, described in chapter 7, frequently go on to a variety of occupations after the streets are behind them. Virginia Bamurange (1998) discovered that street girls in Dar es Salaam, Tanzania, as compared to boys, have limited income opportunities. She reports, "Since earning opportunities are unequal between adolescent boys and girls, street girls mainly provide sexual services as a strategy of survival, while boys . . . improvise several income earning activities, even a kind of career, on the dumping grounds and by serving car owners at hotel areas" (p. 240). Street girls, unlike street boys, are much more vulnerable to physical attack, and our informants do, in fact, frequently report being raped by street boys. There is, in fact, a hierarchy of authority in the streets with the older street boys ruling over the younger street boys and street boys ruling over street girls. Street girls, however, sometimes exercise authority over very young street boys.

Both street girls and boys often have homes of origin characterized by poverty and parental alcoholism. According to our focus group discussions and other interviews, street girls, in comparison to street boys, also experience beatings by parents at their homes of origin. Significantly, it is considered to be quite improper and shameful for a teenage girl to be beaten by her parents ("caned"). For this reason, it is not surprising that a beaten girl would be likely to run and stay away from home. Perhaps for this reason, street girls report very tenuous relations with their families and seem frequently to have little meaningful interaction with them. Street boys, on the other hand, visit home much more often than street girls do, especially to visit their mothers, for whom they take small gifts of money and items such as sugar. Both boys and girls may have friends or acquaintances who introduce them to street life.

For girls, it was our impression that having a child on the streets does present a burden, but at the same time pregnancy and motherhood can be a strategic resource as well. We were struck by the extent to which the child is integrated into the daily round of his mother and also by the degree to which street girls report assistance from other street girls when they are pregnant or have children. We have described earlier why children can be a resource in begging strategies. When we asked what we could do for those who had helped us in a focus group interview, the two pregnant girls in the group, Veronica and Margaret, said immediately that they wanted to have maternity dresses, which we gave to them. Later Veronica posed for us proudly wearing the maternity dress as a cherished memento. It seems while maternity dresses help mothers move about on the streets, they can also have symbolic significance for public and personal identity. In general, the psychological adjustment for some girls while on the streets would suggest that although girls may be coming from harsher home environments than boys, maternity, like paper collection for boys, provides for some of them a means to obtain both resources from enhanced begging opportunities with their babies and gifts from street children, as well as esteem from peers.

In our ethnographic observations we noticed that girls who have infants are assisted whenever possible by their friends. While in transit from place to place, girls will frequently take turns carrying the baby. Food will also be given to the baby when it is available. During one extended visit a street girl, who had been imprisoned with her baby, was visited by her friends, street girls who spent a great deal of time kissing and cooing to the baby while visiting the mother. Our findings of enhanced social solidarity in pregnancy are similar to Virginia Bamurange's (1998) rare published account of pregnant African street girls. She writes for street girls in Dar es Salaam, who survive primarily by prostitution that, "as young and poor as they are, they have forbidden Asia, who is breastfeeding her child, to go on the streets. Instead, they share with her whatever they get. They all contribute to feed the baby" (p. 242).

In our ethnographic research in 1996, Bryn Mawr student Alison Mott summarizes five main reasons why, as street girls reported to her, they became pregnant:

1.   They don't intentionally get pregnant. It's simply that men won't use condoms.
2.   Sex is pleasurable, a way to keep a boyfriend, or a payment for an older boy's protection.
3.   She is raped.
4.   She wants to have babies because babies are valuable in Kenyan culture and a baby will be someone who needs her and will give her a family to belong to.
5.   Babies facilitate more charity for both the mother and the child.

In conclusion, while pregnancy is an experience foreign to many street girls, most have personal involvement such that the risk of pregnancy, frequently undesired and usually in unfavorable circumstances, is more than anything else something that sets off the girls from the boys as a disadvantaged group. Our findings on gender are, on the whole, similar to those of Tobias Hecht (1998), who writes about street children in Brazil as follows:

I believe that, on balance, life in the street tends to be even harder for girls than for boys, not only because of their greater physical vulnerability but also because of social expectations in Brazil about girlhood and boyhood. . . . Girlhood is typically more closely circumscribed, more inimical to the street, more closely allied to the home. (p. 20)

Chapter 9

Suffering on the Streets

The long bench on which the visitors sat held three street girls known to Alison, whose arrival prompted requests for food and concerns over hunger. After a wait, the four companions were escorted inside a locked gate, where in an interior room prisoners were made available to their visitors. A mean-looking, heavy-set, bald guard shouted insults at the three girls. Angel emerged with her infant son, Jimmie, tied on her back. Jimmie was given by his mother to be passed around with the other girls, who kissed and cooed to him. Alison flashed back to three days earlier on a previous visit when she brought bread and milk for Angel and Jimmie. She remembered thinking that jail "stinks like a zoo." Angel looked hungry, angry, and "horribly unhappy" about her plight. On this day, at least, the four visitors were all able to take Jimmie out of jail for awhile. Glancing into the area where prisoners were detained, Alison noted how they were "stuffed like sardines," a fitting metaphor for deplorable prison conditions that all Kenyans agree are to be avoided at all costs. Later, Angel and Jimmie were transferred to a larger, more permanent prison to await further action on her case. It seems that Angel had been reported to the police by a wealthy Kenyan for "setting him up" for a beating and robbery by street children. He had thought that she had agreed to be with him but, in his view, left briefly to inform street boys about all the money he was carrying for them, money to go and have a "good time" together (about 40,000 Kenyan shillings). Angel said that, to the contrary, she had just been talking to the man for the first time when the boys came by and stole his car radio and money after attacking him with a knife on the forehead, then ran away. Some street girls reported to us that Angel was not involved, as the street boys know very well that guys in cars always have money. It is possible that Angel would not know a gang of street boys from some other area of town, while it is also possible that Angel would not report street boys well-known to her. Precisely why a "wealthy man" was seeking to "pick up" a street girl seems to be unproblematic to all parties concerned in this unfortunate episode. (Kilbride and Mott field notes, 1996)

Confinement in jail is described by street children in terms of dreadful living conditions and almost always as having beatings by policemen. In response to our specific questions, one street boy gave the following account concerning his fear of the police:

Q.   What do you fear about being here in the garbage area and around Westlands as a whole?
A.   The police.
Q.   Why?
A.   Because they arrest us, if they find us there at night. They say we are among the kids who beg.
Q.   Where do they take you when they have arrested you?
A.   To jail.
Q.   When was the last time you were arrested by the police? Have you been grabbed by them before?
A.   Yes.
Q.   Where did they take you?
A.   To the juvenile remand.
Q.   When was the last time they grabbed you?
A.   They found me just sitting down.
Q.   When?
A.   Just before this month in late July.
Q.   Then they took you to Juvenile?
A.   Yes, then my mother came over and acknowledged that I was her son and not a beggar.
Q.   What do they do to you there?
A.   They beat us up and make us dig (weed).
Q.   What did your mother do to you?
A.   She had to give them money for them to release me. She gave them Ksh. 600.

ILLNESSES

A medical doctor, who treats street boys in his private clinic in Westlands, described common conditions he treats them for. These include stitches for injuries resulting from fights with other street boys or from the police beatings. Foot cuts are as common since shoes are a luxury. Skin infections are frequent, too, as a result of unsanitary conditions and infrequent bathing. The doctor continued in his interview with us to explain that diarrhea and other intestinal complaints are endemic, as one might expect when garbage is a regular dietary source. Sexually transmitted diseases are seen by him, although he knows of no cases of AIDS or HIV-positive status. In a widely discussed episode among the boys, one boy received a "false" positive result and went into a deep depression, telling other boys that "he would die soon." He was elated for several days after receiving a second and accurate negative result. Respiratory illnesses, such as flu, are common, as is malaria.

In sum, the doctor described the causes behind the medical conditions that he treats as arising from a social scene characterized by the following patterns: (1) unhygenic food from feeding from garbage heaps and unsanitary water; (2) cold weather, exposure from sleeping on pavements, public parks, broken-down vehicles or "houses" of cartons, paper and plastic papers, and cardboard; (3) violence among boys, and (4) unavailability or unwillingness to use condoms. In our observation, however, sex is, for many street boys, unlike girls, fairly infrequent, especially for young boys.

Some boys appear to be in excellent health such as the boy who gave the following testimony in an interview:

Q.   What kind of health problems do you have?
A.   None because it is a must that I bathe.
Q.   Not once have you been ill?
A.   Only colds due to chills at night.
Q.   What about your friends?
A.   Some suffer severe cuts from broken bottles and others from stomach aches.
Q.   When this happens, what do you normally do or from whom do you receive medical help?
A.   There is one mzungu lady. She goes to get a doctor from Aga Khan Hospital who gives us drugs.
Q.   Have you ever heard of AIDS?
A.   AIDS, yes, I have.
Q.   What do you know about AIDS?
A.   I understand you contract it by going with a woman whom you don't know.
Q.   That is all you have heard about AIDS?
A.   Yes, only that.

Clearly, although this young man enjoys good health, he is in need of education about AIDS transmission. His view about its cause is not uncommon.

GLUE

A major health hazard, which our medical consultant emphasized, is glue addiction. Addiction to inhaling glue solvents keeps many boys and girls on the street. Sniffing glue from a small plastic bottle or, for some, inhaling petrol, produces a psychological dependence recognized by social workers and others seeking to rehabilitate street children. Available for a small price, glue is most often obtained from people who make or mend shoes or other street children. Children report a number of recurring reasons for inhaling glue. The most common reasons given are that it suppresses depression, shyness in begging, hunger, and cold (one boy called glue "his blanket").

One boy of about fourteen years stated concerning his use of glue, "when I sniff glue I forget my sufferings. When it is cold, glue helps to maintain my body temperature. I do drink alcohol, too, but I take glue because it is cheap. I stopped using glue because members of the public, especially women, fear street children when they are drunk from glue. This makes people not sympathize with us and give us money." Another boy quit glue because of its physical effects, which he described as like a "hangover," with a headache, lethargy, and general weakness. *Bhangi* is used by some boys along with alcohol, both of which replace the glue bottle by the midteens and later for both boys and girls. Older girls rely primarily on alcohol associated with bars and clubs they frequent in their survival sex work. Girls and boys, but especially girls, frequently in private smoke cigarettes.

Getting money for addictive drug or solvent dependencies is a preoccupation for some children. In the first two years of P. K.'s research in Westlands, for example, his primary informant, Jacob, longed for a new pair of shoes throughout each summer. P. K. noticed after each return that the shoes were nowhere to be seen, and Jacob was again barefooted. It was also P. K.'s impression that Jacob was much more dependent on glue with each passing year. On the third occasion of shoe giving, P. K.'s naivete was eventually lessened when he at last realized that Jacob was selling his shoes for money to buy glue. Other street children revealed this deception to him. Jacob is not unlike many other street boys who beg constantly for shoes, as a careful reading of journalistic accounts and other reports such as our students' notes, personal accounts, and so on clearly indicate.

In 1997, a sociologist colleague visiting Kenya gave a new pair of shoes to a street boy near Kenyatta Market, who quickly sold them for glue money as revealed by follow-up investigation by P. K.'s colleague. It seems that street boys have learned that "wearing shoes" is a middle-class value of some importance, one that has proven to be a significant source of income from middle-class philanthropers. Tragically, it seems clear that the money obtained from shoes goes primarily to maintain glue addiction. For this reason, most perceptive donors give only food and not cash or material items that can be converted into cash. We know of no examples of street girls begging for shoes. In fact, our impression derived from C. S.'s survey-based research and P. K.'s ethnographic work, is that street girls are, on the whole, less given to deception than boys. In our experience this has been so. Perhaps this difference arises in the rather more limited economic opportunities available to them compared to boys, who must use their wits and verbal skills as key ingredients for economic success. Unlike the boys who sold the shoes given to them, the street girls who were given maternity dresses each wore her dress for the remainder of her pregnancy. One still had her dress a year later and even longer, until it was worn out. No exchanges were made for glue.

SURVIVAL SEX AND RAPE

As we noted in the previous chapter, street girls are at the bottom of the status hierarchy on the street, if not in the entire Kenyan society. As such, their young, still-developing bodies and childish smiles may not always immediately reveal what is privately a difficult life of pain and sorrow, one frequently including experiences of sexual exploitation. Certainly we observed many hazards encountered by these girls on a regular basis. We saw, for example, blister sores resulting from embers dropped on bare feet, painful foot lacerations due to stepping on nails, fever from untreated malaria or flu, and toothache. Suffering from harassment (or worse) by some police or internment in jail for extended periods of time, even while pregnant or already a mother with a child, is not uncommon.

As we have seen in the aforementioned case, middle-class men from the suburbs sometimes are a stressful threat to girls when they prostitute themselves. "Going for the road," their expression for survival sex, is nevertheless often a source of income in spite of the risks of diseases and beatings. As one girl put it, "we are treated as rubbish in daytime and as dames at night." Street girls have reported to us other alleged cases in the news media concerning church ministers "marrying" them in exchange for their being given food, although such allegations are difficult to prove.

Perhaps most threatening to the girls is a fear of rape by street boys that is frequently realized in practice. For example, when one of our consultants was asked if street boys disturb her at night, she replied "They do and I even have a scar on my face because I was stabbed by a knife by a boy who wanted to rape me; then I screamed for help." While describing her problems to us, another girl said that, "among other difficulties, we are always being disturbed by our fellows, the street boys especially when you are alone. One could just come where you are sleeping at night to rape you and if you refuse, he threatens you with a knife." Indeed girls in general conversation in response to our inquiries about cuts on their arms and legs often responded that such wounds came from resisting rape. It will be recalled that street girls reported in the focus groups that a major reason for leaving home was being beaten. It is likely that sexual abuse at home is implied on some occasions.

Street boys, for their part, do not generally hold street girls in high regard, some friendships notwithstanding. A key informant expresses a common opinion when he said, "all street girls are prostitutes." Widespread survival sex among street girls poses exposure to HIV as a significant threat to their lives. Girls sometimes use money from sex work for renting houses (for about 300 or

400 shillings a month) in one of the slum areas. Sadly, one girl known to us who practiced survival sex died of AIDS. Her wake in Kayole slums was attended by some of the street boys working with us in Westlands.

PUBLIC VIOLENCE

Street children, especially boys, frequently encounter violence from members of the public that sometimes results in death and injury. In a much-publicized case in 1994, "Simon" was spotted by a police reservist stealing a headlight from a car in the suburbs of Ngara, not far from Westlands. He was shot by the reservist, after which he was dumped in the gutter. The official government response was minimal, with foot dragging almost preventing the eventual arrest of the suspect for trial. We have reported in a previous chapter other cases from the media of seemingly increasing violence involving fellow workers on the street arising from alleged theft or destruction of property by street boys. Other media reports also indicate a clear sense of the social environment of antagonism and violence faced by street children. A recent newspaper article in the *Daily Nation* (April 13, 1998), for example, among many reports of violence, described a fight on Moi Avenue in the city center between a watchman and fellow guards and about 65 street children in which six people were injured and required hospitalization. The fight was set off when, after grabbing a purse from a pedestrian, a fleeing street boy was knocked down by a car. Public response to this incident aptly characterize a growing sense of fear and apprehension about street children. For example, in *The Daily Nation* article just mentioned, the chair lady of the Federation of Women Lawyers said, "these people pose dangers not only to security in various towns but also could discourage tourists visiting our various towns." A spokesperson for a street children relief organization indicated in the same article that a change of attitude was needed because "there has been a lot of stigmatization of the street children to a point where they feel the whole world is against them" (April 13, 1998). In a feature article calling for public sympathy for street children's rights, a Kenyan magazine, *The People*, reported, "Many of us will change direction when we see these street children, warn our children about the *chokora* or pull up our windows preferring to roast in the heat of our own cars (August 1996, p. 2). Another piece in the same publication reported, "The life of the children in the street is tough. You need a rhinoceros hide to survive. Violence is the order of the day. When two groups finally met, hell broke loose. Blows were exchanged, stones, bottles, wood and metal bars tore through the air. Bystanders cowered away" (July 1996, p. 2).

MENTAL ILLNESS AND RETARDATION

Some of the street children are likely to be suffering from mental illness. In our research, the boy mentioned in a previous chapter who interrupted the girl's focus group task while high on glue seemed to be cognitively or mentally impaired. In another case, one day a street boy well-known to P. K. was attracting some attention as he moved about a major street in Westlands. It was at once apparent to P. K. that he was not behaving in the affable manner that normally characterized his demeanor when he was paper collecting or begging. In fact, he was uttering incoherent phrases in an attempt to evoke some reaction, such as fear or sympathy, which might turn up a few shillings from passersby. The boy's nickname, Mcoasti, referred primarily to his home origin but also to his easygoing manner, thought to characterize coastal Kenyans. P. K. was surprised not only by his uncharacteristic behavior on this day, loud and overly aggressive, but also by his dress as well. Mcoasti was shirtless with his body darkened black by charcoal and his hair disheveled in the extreme. P. K. thought to himself that surely Mcoasti had gone mad. This episode recalled a piece on labeling theory in which Douglas Raybeck (1991) points out that deviant behaviors are frequently subject to flexible labels in small groups. None of the street children had previously or subsequently labeled Mcoasti as anything other than "normal," notwithstanding his bizarre behavior on this occasion. Still was Mcoasti "mentally ill" to some extent, or was such behavior entirely socially labeled? All my discussions with him had never produced a hint in my mind of mental disorder, at least in lay terms. In fact, most children, when not on glue, have struck us as quite rational in their overall behavior, although there are variations of personality or character dispositions, and some children come across as more articulate than others, perhaps suggesting differences in intelligence. In our focus group research, we encountered one girl who struck us as being cognitively challenged, and it is likely that instances of mental retardation have been observed by others who work closely with Nairobi's street children. Patricia Wolford, for example, writes in the *Plain Dealer* of her work in Nairobi, "A retarded girl about 14 years of age came to our lunch program on the street. . . . There was only one organization that had 24-hour care for the mentally retarded, but it was for rich families" (September 27, 1996, p. 12b). Overall, cases of mental retardation notwithstanding, survival on the street is, itself, a testimony to the cognitive adaptability, even a degree of invulnerability, of most street children observed by us.

Chapter 10

Applied: Multiple Strategies, Cultural Solutions, and the Way Forward

I greeted my old friend warmly as we embraced after several years of separation. Dr. Rick Thompson, anthropologist/ missionary, with his wife, Cheri, were running a project for former street children (and other poor children) to provide for them an opportunity to manufacture items for sale. The main item sold in large quantities was brown paper bags decorated with animal prints such as zebra and elephant. Rick expressed enthusiasm for their project, itself part of a larger educational effort including a school, a library, and Christian education. Nevertheless, he was concerned that efforts at "rehabilitation" of street children were problematic because of the scarcity of jobs in Kenya after vocational training. For the short term, however, the paper bag work was run as a cooperative and, as such, the project teaches valuable social skills such as teamwork, planning, and saving for the future. In fact, he pointed out to me that he was wary of most "rehabilitation" efforts, believing that by now most kids have had a chance to get off the streets but are not given ample opportunity to get money except through begging and handouts. He thinks too that, by and large, street children see through often hypocritical church policies aimed at handouts in exchange for church loyalty. All in all, he believes that prevention should be the objective in future efforts to address the street children problem, he concluded with conviction. I asked, after returning to the subject of street children from discussions about the need for spiritual solutions to some social problems in the United States, if he ever gets "depressed" because clearly all efforts to correct the known conditions responsible for street children had not succeeded, as he had pointed out in his own observation above. Rick responded "no," it was the lot of people like me to search for social solutions so as to "repair" society whereas for him his "spiritual" concern takes each individual child as a special and unique person worthy of special attention. (Kilbride, 1997, field notes)

P. K. asked his companion what he thought about street children. He expressed an opinion shared by many urban Kenyan homeowners and others with a stake in the system that street children were on the street by parental choice. He pointed out that parents are to be blamed for sending their children out to the street to beg so as to obtain money for them. In his view, poverty has absolutely nothing to do with the increasing number of street children; rather the only solution to this "menace" is to discipline parents. "White-collar" citizens, like the agent, often agree with a standard government response, shared also by news media friendly to government policies, that street children are self-chosen to a great extent. This defensive view is perhaps understandable to some extent, given that many members of the public often exclusively turn to the government for a "solution." P. K. suggested to him, however, that any solution to the problem of street children is complex, far more so than singular explanations, such as family and child deception or government inaction, although these factors are implicated. (Kilbride field notes, 1997)

Attempted solutions to the problems of street children in Kenya abound in numerous governmental, NGO, church and private programs specifically concerned with rehabilitation and preventative programs. Still, in spite of goodwill and expensive programs, the street children population continues to grow along with an increasing consensus that rehabilitation programs have not proven to be effective. Instead, programs are now addressing preventive strategies designed, for example, to intervene not directly with street children but instead at the family level to enhance the family's capacities to better cope with the social and economic factors well-known to contribute to the movement of children from homes to the street in the first place (Suda, 1999). More rarely now do programs or private individuals give money directly to street children for fear that such gifts will be converted into glue or other substances.

Currently in Kenya, interventions stress both rehabilitation and prevention with a focus on community-based organizations (CBOs) empowered with resources to provide money not directly to the child, but rather support for schooling, training for employment, and recreational activities such as sports, art, and music. The child is by and large nowadays understood as an active agent, one who must be motivated to participate willingly in his own rehabilitation. Attempts, for example, to forcibly relocate street children into "homes" have not worked. Instead, street children overall flee from such institutions, where disciplinary regimes and required labor are emphasized. Nevertheless, programs that do conform to a concept of family and child reciprocal interactions frequently are less effective than one might hope; but this is understandable, given the limited resources and sheer numbers of available programs. There is much overlap and duplication of effort, which is further exacerbated by distinct levels of social organization, often with incompatible assumptions and knowledge bases about street children and their aspirations. International, national, and local programs of intervention and prevention are often active without vertical linkages and sometimes without any shared cultural assumptions about causes, solutions, and other ideas pertaining to the overall social environment within which the street child and his family operate.

In the pages to follow we will develop a holistic model for intervention, one that recognizes the existence of "levels" of social organization pertaining to applied programs for street children. We will propose better coordination of programs within and between levels in this chapter. We believe that the following levels can be identified: the child; his family; the community of local street children; adults regularly involved in social rehabilitation (NGOs, social workers, church groups); Kenyan national institutions (e.g., police, justice system, Child Welfare Society); and international programs (e.g., United Nations, church missionary programs).

All of these levels work in partnership, and each partner is a stakeholder. We will also recommend here the relevance of a "cultural model" for application to the Kenyan national level. The special place of Kenyan ideas about the extended family will be emphasized. There is "within" level variation and, therefore, a need for horizontal linkage also recognized by us. At the level of the street child, for example, the significance of gender difference is crucial. At the Kenyan national level, the Child Welfare Society differs considerably from the Kenyan police in a variety of assumptions about the place of physical force in the treatment of street children.

In sum, in this chapter, we will organize our description of existent programs and our own specific applied recommendations around the concept of levels of social organization, within level variation and the need for better integration both across and within levels. Given the significance of the extended family and related institutions compared, for instance, to Europe and America, where outside funding programs largely originate, we emphasize the important place for a cultural model for enhanced international understanding in the arena of street children advocacy in Kenya.

LEVELS OF SOCIAL ORGANIZATION

A need to recognize levels of distinct but interacting domains of social phenomena that shape events in Africa is argued persuasively in a comprehensive review article by York Bradshaw, Paul Kaiser and Stephen Ndegua (1995). They state that studies of developmental change, for example, need to examine (1) the interaction between the global, national, and local levels and (2) the interaction among factors within each level. They also cite, among other examples, explanations for the problems of food security in Africa to illustrate their model. Global explanations are given of such things as the declining price for raw materials. National level explanation focuses on such factors as failed government programs and inefficient state farms whereas local explanations consider, for example, inadequate resources in the community such as land, fertilizer, and credit. Within level factors operate on all these levels (see

p. 39). For example, Bradshaw, Kaiser, and Ndegua (1995) write, "numerous organizations and institutions also attempt to mobilize national level support to enact change. Labor organizations, churches, political parties, and women's groups are only a few organizations that shall be considered" (p. 43). Thus, famine in Africa cannot be eliminated unless interactions across and within levels are considered simultaneously and not separately, as is common at present.

As mentioned above, we believe that a full understanding of street children intervention programs requires following the concept of levels of social organization. We also believe that their model, specifically intended for Africa, requires the addition of a "family level" given the importance of the family, specifically the extended family in social life throughout the continent. This is especially relevant for programs for children, including street children. In fact, Bradshaw, Kaiser, and Ndegua (1995) intend their inductive model to be "grounded" in specific cultural context and therefore subject to the sort of adjustment proposed here by us for application in Kenya and perhaps elsewhere in Africa where family values are significant (p. 45).

Levels: Vertical Linkages

Early attempts to assist street children in Kenya were frequently motivated by good will, charitable, and other humanitarian motives. Street children were seen almost entirely as victims with no agency of their own, such as a capacity to figure out appropriate strategies to maximize benefits to be gained by manipulating those seeking to help them. In short, there was little vertical linkage between donors' motives and those of the children perceived by them exclusively as "victims." Previously, we have documented the consequences of giving shoes, for example, which are often converted to glue or again begging strategies that sometimes maximize misfortune. Current thinking about intervention strategies generally reflect a tighter vertical fit between the child as an active participant with a keen sense of multiple survival strategies, including frequent manipulation of public community level benefactors.

A recent article in the *Daily Nation* (Jan. 14, 1998, p. 3) about Childlife Trust, established in Kenya in 1993 to assist street children, illustrates improved vertical linkage. The Childlife Trust Board "comprises community leaders. After exploring possible avenues for assisting these children, they came to an unusual conclusion: 'Do not give hand outs—money, bread, sweets, clothes, shoes to children begging in the streets.' " The *Daily Nation* article continues to point out that Childlife Trust believes the handouts make the streets more appealing than school and home, while also encouraging adults to send children to the streets to beg. Glue is also often purchased with money received in handouts. As an alternative to direct gifts of money, Childlife Trust encourages donations of money and time to organizations working with street children.

Volunteering to help in teaching and sports coaching, for instance, is advocated as well as material donations such as blankets, toys, and used clothing.

An international organization, Feed the Children, illustrates vertical linkage with national and local levels of social organizations. A significant application of a cultural perspective is also evident in adjustments made by Feed the Children to be better in touch with social realities "on the ground" in Kenya. Feed the Children began in 1985 in Kenya as a program initiated by an American based church ministry (Larry Veronica Ministries) introduced in Kenya by the African Inland Church. While Feed the Children began by providing direct assistance to the street children on the streets "its mission is now re-focusing, with empowerment of women now gaining more currency says Paul Sungut, the Country Director" (*Daily Nation*, 1998: Caleb Muchungu). Feed the Children now organizes mothers in slums into groups who open a bank account. Each member makes a small contribution each month in exchange for large loans made available to members in cycles. This "merry-go-round" concept is a familiar one in Kenya, where "group membership" is a means for mutual savings for self- and family improvement in housing, child education, and now street children prevention by dealing first with the economic problems that contribute to the movement of street children from home in the first place. Group members use loans to enhance their businesses such as selling clothes or groceries or managing kiosks. The Feed the Children Credit program director, Gabriel Mukanga, states, "The idea is to empower women such that they are able to run their small business better and therefore offer a better living standard to their children" (*Daily Nation*, January 11, 1998).

It is noteworthy that the Feed the Children intervention program recognizes the importance of the mother–child relationship within the broader cultural value context of African family. Feed the Children, it should be emphasized, does not only provide credit for women whose children can benefit before they turn to the street. Feed the Children also sponsors street children rehabilitation centers. We visited one such center in Mukuru–Reuben Village located in the industrial area. Here we undertook a community profile investigation through personal visits that revealed the following information.

The village holds an unusually large population of about 15,000 people. Many residents of Mukuru-Reuben work in the adjacent industrial area in factories such as those that make garments. Many others are casual laborers who seek employment wherever possible in the city. Many in the community are Kamba by ethnicity, having migrated from the Machakos area to Nairobi in search of employment. Children residing here on the whole express little curiosity when Europeans visit their village, indicating a higher level of exposure to Kenyan society as compared, for example, to the children of Korogocho described earlier. The visitor is struck by the extent to which the community is very spacious, with some of the households having gardens that give a kind of rural ambience to the community in comparison to Korogocho and other slum areas described previously. The rate of population growth is very high because the village has grown into a major source of cheap labor for surrounding industrial enterprises. The village also accommodates unemployed youth, single mothers, broken and neglected families, and many social outcasts. The average household size is 7.5 persons, most of whom are crowded into small houses. Housing in Mukuru-Reuben village is typical of poor urban communities in Nairobi. The majority of the structures have timber walls and concrete or earth floors. Other houses have mud walls or are primarily made up of plastic materials and cartons. Some of the villagers own the structures they occupy and rent out others. There is a scarcity of clean water for domestic consumption. Piped water can be purchased at 3 Ksh. per 20 liter jerry can. Public health services including drainage, sanitation, and waste disposal are poor. The area has no bathrooms, and people bathe either in their small rooms or in the open at night. Fecal disposal is poor, with poorly maintained communally used pit latrines, a single one of which is used by as many as over ten families.

The objectives of Feed the Children Program (FCP) in Mukuru-Reuben include provision of food, clothing, education, and health services for the community's children, some of whom are former street children, as a way of reducing chances of their going to or returning to the streets in search of survival alternatives. The FCP sponsors a street child's rehabilitation center housed in the village, and the center cares for about 40 former street children. It has built housing structures for the children equipped with sleeping rooms, a dining hall, and well-maintained pit latrines.

We made a visit to the rehabilitation center and were shown around by its director. The center has two small buildings with iron sheet roofing. One building has office space and cooking facilities, and special food for malnourished children is prepared here along with standard Kenyan food. The other building contains sleeping quarters for the boys and for supervisors. A separate room has two beds for older boys, which is a privilege resulting from their seniority. A separate room is a sign of their elder status, which requires that they discipline the younger boys and make sure that they behave, watch out for glue use, and maintain discipline. Another bedroom contains several beds for the younger and older boys who are not leaders. A third sleeping area has a large common mattress available for men who are employed to work with the boys. Twenty-four boys are housed and fed in the rehabilitation center. These children are schooled locally at a school to which Feed the Children donated a building. Two girls have recently joined the program; each has a brother currently at the rehabilitation center.

The children at the center all have kinsmen living in Mukuru-Reuben and are therefore of the community itself. At a meeting called by Feed the Children, community leaders were asked about their viewpoints about the rehabilitation center. In general, they are supportive but noted that some of the street children were bad influences and responsible for introducing glue to the community, for instance. The leaders also felt that food and shelter were not enough, that the children needed clothing as well.

A CULTURAL MODEL: FOSTERING

As mentioned above, Feed the Children builds upon available cultural resources such as the importance in Kenya of children as members of families and the widespread importance attached to the collective, mutual benefit of voluntary associations. We believe that there is merit for further thinking about how indigenous kinship mechanisms might serve to reduce the number of street children on the streets or at risk of moving there. We discussed in an earlier chapter the cultural significance of kinship fostering in Kenya, noting the widespread practice of sending children to be raised by relatives for various reasons. We also noted how grandmothers are especially burdened these days by often reluctantly taking on the role of provider for these grandchildren born, for example before marriage or orphaned by AIDS. We believe that with proper financial assistance and innovative organization, however, that kinship fostering could be the basis for reducing street children or those at risk of becoming street children.

Indeed, one organization that we will discuss later that is specifically concerned with the rehabilitation of street girls, Rescue Dada, has already successfully applied a kinship-based solution in at least a small number of cases. Rescue Dada, founded in 1991, specializes in the rescue, rehabilitation, and reintegration of street girls. At their rehabilitation center in Nairobi, girls are provided with shelter, food, and informal education, but reintegration is the ultimate objective. According to Wairimu Ndirangu of Rescue Dada, "In some cases we travel deep into the countryside to establish contacts with the families of the girls and so begin the reintegration process." In one successful case Dr. Ndirangu reports, "Sarah is now 5 years old and very happy. We first met Sarah begging when she was 3 years old. She had been 'trained' to beg by her grandmother (a 38-year-old prostitute) . . . at the center we discovered that Sarah had been raped and burnt with cigarettes. . . . We were able to contact her other grandmother, a difficult task as she lives 200 kms. from Nairobi, who was overjoyed, believing the child to be dead. Sarah now lives with her, and she recently started school."

Mrs. Joyce Umbima, formerly of the Child Welfare Society of Kenya, is an advocate of kinship fostering (see Grant, 1991, p. 3), which has been strained by changes in Kenya such as "massive poverty, uncontrolled population growth and the new phenomenon of single parenthood." Umbima feels that kinship fostering, which was built into indigenous culture as a means for caring for weak and disadvantaged children, is still significantly present in rural Kenya today.

Fostering is sometimes observed among street children beyond Kenya. Lewis Aptekar (1988), in his study of street children from Cali, Colombia, pointed out that among these children fostering relationships were sometimes initiated by the child rather than the adult. In such cases the child must convince the adult that he or she can be of value to the latter. For example, Aptekar (1988) described the enterprise of one child who always slept near the garage of a wealthy family until they felt that they must indeed do something about him. The man suggested that they might need him to guard their house, so it was agreed to let him sleep inside the garage in exchange for this service. Gradually, he became part of their group of workers, enabling him to receive more benefits such as food. In other cases, street children were informally adopted because they looked like a young relative who had died or because the benefactors had once been street children themselves (Aptekar, 1988, p. 40).

Family breakdown and an increased inability of extended families to serve as support networks for orphaned and other children in deprived or difficult circumstances has been well documented in Kenya (see Kilbride & Kilbride, 1990; Suda, 1997; Weisner, Bradley, & Kilbride, 1997). Such processes as rapid urbanization, high population growth rate, changing expectations of marriage, poverty, and costly requirements for child support and schooling have all played a role in Kenya's changing family culture and structure. The current significance attached to the nuclear family and monogamy as opposed to the indigenous values of extended family and polygyny has also been significant (Kilbride, 1994; Suda, 1999).

Still, the extended family ideology has proven very resilient and adaptive over time and, thus, even with change remains as a viable and dynamic presence in one form or another in the lives of most Kenyans (Weisner, Bradley, & Kilbride, 1997). It is this family dynamism that we feel has considerable potential in helping to address the problems of how to rehabilitate some street children in circumstances where family members can be located. Adoption of nonrelatives is quite rare in Kenya and not a practical alternative at this point. If it is agreed that kinship fostering is a reasonable solution in some cases, then suitable mechanisms for application would need to be set up. Money for locating relatives and provisions for the maintenance and schooling of fostered street children would be required. In addition, social workers to evaluate and oversee the home placements would be needed.

Nevertheless, what are the social and economic costs of doing nothing different than perpetuating current programs? In spite of current policies and programs, even with some modification, the number of street children continues to rise. Indeed, a good case can be made that all current programs collectively serve to perpetuate the problem rather than to reduce the number of street children and improve the quality of their lives. Studying American homelessness historically, Kim Hopper and Jim Baumohl (1994) believe a formally aggressive "abeyance" process by state and NGOs has in recent decades become, as it were, mere warehousing in shelters. Reduced to a single function of social control, the abeyance process now serves primarily to reproduce rather than alleviate homelessness in the United States. Likewise, recent practices in Kenya, such as simply giving money directly to street children and programs that are not culturally sensitive, are good examples of an ineffective "abeyance" process at work in Kenya. Such policies serve to warehouse children on the streets. As a new policy, perhaps grandmothers in Kenyan villages could be organized into associations for care of grandchildren, which might include some of the economic "merry-go-round" strategies described above, thus empowering grandmothers economically to help themselves and their families. Additional supplements for education and maintenance would also be required, of course. Probably kinship solutions would be most suitable for children of a young age as the example above from the Rescue Dada intervention.

A kinship solution, however, cannot be the only plan for intervention or even the major one. We will discuss other applications below. Social conditions favorable for the extended family have changed dramatically. Practices such as brideprice payment, patriarchy, polygyny, wife inheritance, and circumcision ceremonies that served to reinforce the extended family ideology are nowadays contested practices. Nevertheless, we do not believe that such "traditional" customs, even in modified forms, are necessarily "essential" outcomes of an extended family ideology. We believe that family institutions can, to a great extent, be "invented" in response to changing circumstances (Kilbride, 1994).

HORIZONTAL INTEGRATION: GENDER

As noted above, levels of social organization have both vertical and horizontal dimensions. Within-level analysis is also relevant to our search for reduction, if not amelioration, of the problems of street children in Kenya. Better coordination of international programs within Kenya from various nations with contrasting political philosophies, enhancing integration of national, state, and church programs in Kenya, and seeking to eliminate NGO overlap at the community level are just a few examples of needed better horizontal integration in the social organization of street children rehabilitation programs. At the level of the child (and family) gender is arguably the most significant variable, certainly the one that arises in our own research.

A cultural perspective notwithstanding, wide agreement exists that girls compared to boys are disadvantaged in indigenous and contemporary Kenyan society. Rape, wife beating, forced circumcision, unwanted wife inheritance, for example, are all aspects of social life in Kenya. Interpretations of such practices as being harmful to some women are complicated by evidence that women themselves frequently approve of these and other such practices. It cannot be denied that women also have considerable resources for respect and power, especially in domains associated with family life. At the same time, there can be no doubt that men enjoy more social power in public and family life as compared to women (Kilbride & Kilbride, 1990). This gender disparity is reproduced on the streets, as we have noted previously.

While we have suggested that "family solutions" are to be encouraged in Kenya, we caution that such solutions be particularly mindful regarding reintegration of children into families, which can be especially burdensome to street girls compared to boys and to women compared to men. We noted previously how street boys in our study, more regularly than girls, visit home. Girls report being severely beaten at home, where rape is an added general hazard compared to boys. So a decision for a girl to leave home is indeed a more extreme one than for boys. This makes girls vulnerable when rehabilitated to families unless special attention is given to their situation. Having a baby before marriage can be a source of considerable family consternation for a girl but not for a boy in Kenya today as compared to previous generations when monogamy was not valued over the extended family and all children were accepted as family members. Sending a girl with a baby home to a relative would not only be an added expense but might also expose a girl to punishment by some relatives for her "embarrassing" behavior.

Infanticide is now a not infrequent practice in Kenya (Kilbride, 1991). School girls, for example, who became pregnant are usually dismissed from school permanently while little attention is given to school boys or men who impregnate secondary school students. In one case of attempted infanticide reported by Philip Kilbride (1992), the student gave birth in the school dormitory and attempted to kill her baby by throwing him into a latrine. The baby did not die, but the mother and her baby were detained in jail for some days until the baby's survival was assured. In sum, thereafter, mother and child were placed on court probation for three years under the supervision of the former student's mother. The girl's maternal uncle and brother helped the student to overcome her crisis through jail visits, bail, money, and encouragement, thereby showing the role of the extended family in crisis. Nevertheless, the family was embarrassed by the whole affair. Kilbride (1992) writes concerning the brother's view of his sister's plight:

We want to get the entire matter resolved before it gets on the radio or newspaper. Our family's reputation will be affected. The whole matter could have been avoided if the police were not involved in the first place. After all, the baby did not die. Yes, the headmaster made it unnecessarily complicated. I want to get my sister out of jail as soon as possible. Moreover, so far, she has been slapped by the police only once but, overall, they have been fine. (p. 125)

It might be argued that prevention rather than rehabilitation should be emphasized in the future so as to avoid the complexities associated with rehabilitation, especially by the use of family-based solutions for street girls who have children. This would certainly be the case for children over 10 years old. A family solution for both boys and girls, of course, need not force children "back home" into somewhat authoritarian family structures where abuse of power sometimes occurs. We have noted above that the majority of children from poor families do not turn to the streets (Suda, 1997). Certainly some children, especially girls, are escaping oppressive family structures, especially exacerbated by alcoholism and "delocalized polygyny" (Kilbride & Kilbride, 1990) where relatively impoverished men have taken on too many wives without the capacity to support them. Nevertheless, we believe that as a starting premise, rehabilitative strategies for boys and girls should begin first by considering the positive outcomes made possible by seeking to rehabilitate children as members of family structures, ones that themselves need to be strengthened as part of policy.

Programs specifically for girls are currently available in Kenya and deserve to be strengthened. The Mukuru school, for example, is located in a slum area by that name. It serves girls only, from 7 to 17, half of whom used to be street children. Mary Killeen, an Irish Sister of Mercy, founded this school in 1985. In addition to academics, girls are taught practical skills like sewing and knitting. Killeen cautions that many of the young women remain vulnerable. "It is very easy for a middle class fellow to come and buy chips for a girl here and pretend he loves her," she says. "The girl is left with no hope, just despair, and maybe a baby as well" (*Christian Science Monitor*, April 3, 1998, p. 6). Sister Killeen states, "Now to see those girls just laughing . . . doing very well in school . . . is one of the most wonderful things." Mukuru benefits from vertical linkage. The Kenyan government provides this community-level school, one "horizontally" specialized to serve girls, with salaries for some teachers while global linkage comes from the United Nation's World Food Program, which furnishes hot lunches.

We have previously described how pregnancy affects the lives of street girls in our study. Rescue Dada Center takes in street girls ranging from newborns up to sixteen years. Some of the children of the girls in our street research were living at Rescue Dada. Some babies at the center are HIV positive. Global integration with Rescue Dada includes a robust element of volunteerism. Ndirangu (1994) writes, "We depend on donor funds and well wishers . . . groups of well wishers especially in Germany and other European countries organize themselves and send us used clothes, books (for informal schooling), toys and fabric (for tailoring projects" (p. 2). We have seen how pregnancy can sometimes be an asset for street girls. There is some risk that support groups like Rescue Dada make it easier for some girls who profit by having their babies and thereby actually serve to encourage pregnancies in some cases. I. Susser (1996), in a review article about homelessness and poverty in U.S. cities, discusses studies that show that having children sometimes gives poor women an advantage over poor men and childless women such that "homeless women without children excluded from services for women with children are likely to be the most brutalized group of all" (p. 421). Susser believes that early pregnancy might be an asset for girls in some situations with limited options in impoverished environments.   Nevertheless, our research indicates that expectation of economic gains in begging and enhanced sociality are only two reasons recognized by girls themselves as encouraging pregnancy. Most pregnancies are unplanned, and a significant number of girls are raped. Under the present circumstances, Rescue Dada and similar organizations should, in our judgment, be strongly supported.

There are currently many more programs for boys than girls. This is not surprising since there are many more street boys than street girls (about 80% are boys). One of the first and well-established organizations working with street boys is the Undugu Society of Kenya. The word *undugu* in Kiswahili means brotherhood, an apt term for one of the first welfare societies established in Kenya devoted to the rehabilitation of street boys. The Undugu program was established through the work of Father Arnold Grol, a missionary. His street children project began with an effort in 1975 to assist the parking boys by incorporating them into his programs in the slums of Mathare Valley to help young boys who were idle at home. In the 1970s, the Undugu Society grew rapidly into a welfare structure for poor boys including youth clubs with recreational activities such as art, drama, and a popular band known as the Undugu Beat 75. Basic skills taught in the Undugu vocational training center include, among others, carpentry, masonry, tailoring, and shoemaking. A basic education program was set up for school dropouts and ex–parking boys with sponsorship for school fees, uniforms, and shoes. Today the Undugu Society has extended its projects to include girls, beginning with an effort in the 1980s to assist prostitutes.

In our focus group research discussed in chapter 5, we found that a willingness to work at *karatasi* (paper collection) is a salient aspiration for street boys in our study. Currently, street boys work as individuals and are individually subjected to the vagaries of market demand and exploitation by buyers, rainy season shutdowns, and physical injury risks, for example, by handling sharp objects. Older boys sometimes have an advantage over younger boys by virtue of their strength and ability to form alliances with *askaris* at places where large supplies of waste products have accumulated.

There is a conceptual need to recognize that street boys are in many ways best thought about as members of the "working poor" social class so as to maximize benefits for the boys. We suggest that it would be useful to plan how best to organize street boys into work cooperatives to better ensure that their labor, which is now largely unrecognized in the significant area of garbage collection, is in the future better renumerated so as to maximize benefits for the children. The "Hearing on Street Children in Kenya" report (1995, p. 32) has also called for public, private and international organizations to encourage street children to organize into units for garbage recycling. Children under 14 are not supposed to work in Kenya, although many paper collectors are under this age. Nevertheless, most of the paper collectors in our research were 14 and over, the younger ones specializing in begging or helping to guard cars. A *karatasi* work cooperative worked out in conformity with Kenya's labor laws for children would reduce exploitation and maximize profits for the children themselves.

Experienced middlemen and women, such as Mama Ford discussed earlier, are often well liked by the children and could be recruited to help organize street children in cooperatives. Nevertheless, not all middle persons are to be trusted and careful assessment would be required before this involvement in shared work projects with street children.

Based on our research and following the "Hearing on Street Children in Kenya" report (1995, p. 19), we strongly believe that formal education should be made available for every child in Kenya, boys and girls. Education and job training were clear and consistent aspirations of the boys and girls in our study. Applied solutions in order to have a maximum chance for success must recognize the children's aspirations. To enhance this objective was the main reason we decided to undertake focus group discussions with street children themselves. Judging by our results, the best way to assist street children is to come into compliance with the International Labour Organization's principle 138, which requires that every child in the world is to be provided with compulsory, free, and universal education. In Kenya this ideal has been frustrated through a reduction of public commitment to universal education in place of a reliance on "cost-sharing" strategies. The materials needed for school attendance discussed in our chapter on Nairobi show clearly that dropout rates speak for themselves about the failure of present policy to achieve anything remotely approaching universal school attendance once available in Kenya. There is clearly a need here for a public debate about prioritizing national developmental goals if universal education is to be reestablished in Kenya.

There is sufficient wealth in Kenya to provide universal education for all children. Donor funds now targeted directly for street children might arguably be better spent on prevention through diversion into public funds for universal education. This would include cost for books, uniforms, school lunches and related costs in addition to fees. Whether or not jobs are available for children who leave school is a related but different issue. The school years are themselves a potential time of learning and fun. No street child should miss out on school, seen as one stage in the life cycle. In any case, the street children themselves speak loudly and consistently about the importance of being in school although some have run away from school on their own. Most had no alternative but to leave school.

COMMUNITY LEVEL

Many other programs like Mukuru, Rescue Dada, and Undugu described above also operate at the community level, often with links both nationally and internationally. There is a strong emphasis in Kenya on the CBO for applied projects including those directed at street children. NGOs face a number of recurring challenges. There is a widespread and continuing effort by NGOs to raise resources. International programs and benefactors remain a constant pool of potential benefactors, although increasingly efforts are made to develop internal measures for generating income.

We need to assess NGOs for longitudinal effectiveness. Virtually everyone has success stories to tell about rehabilitation. There are cases of street boys who have gone on to become university graduates, prosperous businessmen and women, teachers, and other respected members of society. The smaller number wind up in jail or as con artists.

Our material presented earlier shows that many street boys known to Mama Ford and to us are now struggling to make a transition into a steady means of gaining a livelihood. In addition to the prevention of street life, this transition at about 18 to 20 years of age should receive top priority in intervention strategies. Far less is known about street girls, but it is clear that girls have more hurdles to overcome in rehabilitation and must face with other Kenyan women difficult circumstances for upward mobility. Girls, as we have noted, are taken out of school before boys in circumstances of family poverty. Those teenage Kenyan girls who became unwed mothers generally face school expulsion and family and community stigma, as we have noted. There is no doubt that short-term results in rehabilitation are clearly evident in some of the materials reviewed in this chapter. Nevertheless, most activists complain of recidivism as a marked and most discouraging pattern, whereas most of the street boys in our Westlands study are no longer on the streets after six years. Street girls Wanjiru, Veronica, and Margaret are still on the streets, although they are no longer living in Jevanjee Gardens.

CHURCH PROGRAMS

Many of the community-grounded programs are church sponsored. Such programs, however, usually have significant national and even international linkages. We mentioned the Roman Catholic–based Undugu Society previously. The Anglican Church at All Saints Cathedral runs a program where the street girls from Jevanjee Gardens join other street children at the church grounds several days a week for free food and other material gifts. Bishop Manases Kuria, the former archbishop of the Church of the Province of Kenya (CPK), founded a program to set up Christian homes for street children. Bishop Kuria's philosophy is primarily spiritual, drawing its inspiration from the Christian gospel. The name of his organization, "Jehovah Jireh Christian Homes," in the Luo language means "God provides."

Recently, Bishop Kuria was interviewed at a *harambee* (let's pull together) public fund raising for his programs. This interview, reported in an article by Mbothu Kamau in the newspaper *The People* provides a good illustration of Bishop Kuria's spiritual approach to resolving the street children problem in Kenya. Kuria said in his interview that "It is pointless to say that Kenyans are a God-fearing people if the rich in the country continue to accumulate vast sums of money while the underprivileged section of the population goes hungry, walk naked, and sleep in the open" (August 1996 Feature Section). Bishop Kuria advocates national self-reliance, with some help from international donors as indicated in the following remark: "We can get enough clothes in Kenya without begging from overseas. We can also get food and education right from within, only that the well-to-do have no time to think about the under-privileged (August 1996 Feature Section)." Bishop Kuria ultimately blames the problem of street children on excessive capitalism in Kenya, which encourages corruption, greed, and selfishness. He emphasizes too a general drift from African socialism, which he believes to be more community sensitive than the individualism promoted in capitalism. The *Hearing on Street Children in Kenya* report (1995) also considers excessive affluence to be a problem in efforts to help street children. This report states, "The well-to-do members of our society, on their part, will have to agree to forego the affluence to which they have been accustomed. We must agree to make do with less in order to uplift the standards of the disadvantaged in our society" (p. 11). Some well known, very successful community programs associated with Bishop Kuria's efforts include the St. Nicholas Home in Karen and Mama Ngina home for children in South C.

Spiritual-based solutions above, of course, cannot resolve Kenya's problem with street children. Although Kenya is indeed a nation with a profound spiritualism, such sentiments are not necessarily universalistic; nor do all churches assume an activist role vis-a-vis children. Haverford College student Marie Horchler (n.d.), working with Philip Kilbride, interviewed pastors in Nairobi in 1993 concerning their opinions about church involvement or lack thereof in uplifting street children. She found variation such that however admirable Bishop Kuria's stance is in our eyes, it seems that his activist viewpoint is not widespread among churchmen. She found in her interviews with six pastors mixed viewpoints on the issue of activism. One minister felt the government should do more and that it was not the churches' role to prod them to action. Another felt the government should do more and that the church should encourage the government. All felt that family morals had to be improved, and some gave sermons from time to time about street children. One pastor in particular distanced himself and his church from any involvement with street children. He said in his interview with Horchler:

The efforts which have been made to help street children such as feeding and clothing programs only result in well-fed and better-clothed street children. He compared this situation to the welfare system in America, which only encourages people to be dependent on the society as a way of living. In other words, if you keep giving food and clothing, then the mothers of these children will keep sending them out to get these handouts. He also discussed work ethics and said that he would gladly give money to someone for sweeping around the church yard or washing the car instead of giving money to those who just beg. In his opinion, people have become more dependent on society and less self-reliant as happened in the American welfare system. (Horchler, 1993)

In spite of variation in church-based spiritual commitments to assist street children, for those who do value church based intervention, the anecdote at the start of this chapter raises a good point. According to a spiritual perspective, every child helped is a positive outcome, even if "the system" remains intact in spite of spiritual appeals by Bishop Kuria and others to the contrary.

On the problematic side, there is also a danger that church-based programs may be overly concerned with conversion objectives rather than universalistic "love based" spiritualism mixed with African socialism advocated by Bishop Kuria and others. For example, according to a report in the *Daily Nation* by Arthur Okwembah (June 5, 1998, p. 28), some feeding programs supported by the NGO Plan International support children who are in attendance at informal religion lessons initiated by an American missionary couple. Their feeding program is meant only for children who are in attendance at Bible lessons, as well as providing them with stationery for the lessons. In spite of the best of intentions, "the success of their efforts is stifled with sectarian differences . . . the Muslims restrain their children from joining the Christians during meals, fearing that the rites that precede may be intended to convert them. Such beliefs leave the Muslim children hungry, although they attend the lessons" (p. 23).

It is our impression that although we have encountered Muslim street children in Nairobi, strong religious values in Islam may have served to lessen the number of street children in Mombasa where Islam is the dominant religion. P. K. spent several days in old Mombasa, which is almost exclusively Muslim, where he systematically visited marketplaces every morning to seek out street children. Not a single child begged from him, though there were many children on the streets, and it was clear that he was a potentially wealthy visitor. A Muslim, female storeowner on Moi Avenue in central Mombasa offered her own assessment of fewer "parking boys" in Mombasa as compared to Nairobi. She said those in Mombasa come primarily from Nairobi and elsewhere up country. Some of these have run away from an approved school in Lokoni, near Mombasa. These boys, she said, teach local boys about glue. Street boys in Mombasa collect *karatasi,* inhale glue, and frequently ask her for work. She has not seen street girls in Mombasa. She believes there are few street children in Mombasa other than primarily outsiders because the family unit is so strong and there is a tradition of helping the poor in Islam. Other informants reported that street children and other beggers can be seen gathering around mosques on Friday for alms. After several days in Mombasa, P. K. was able to see some street children for himself, some of whom begged from him, including boys as well as a woman with a baby on her back. Street children also scavenge at waste dumps on the outskirts of the city (see Bambrah, 1996). In general, there are street children in Mombasa similar to those in Nairobi, but their presence is not evident in old Mombasa, where Islam is strongest.

EXPRESSIVE CULTURE

African street children, like their counterparts elsewhere, number many who display artistic skills (Swart, 1990). Kenya is no exception. Some programs seek to address the "whole" child by developing ways to involve children in art, music, and theatrical performances. One project centered in the community where our ethnographic research occurred was the Westlands Children Ministries, founded in 1993 by an American, Patricia Wolford. Beth Swadener, a child psychologist, has published material on Westlands Ministries, where she worked as a volunteer in the course of her own research on early childhood education in Kenya. Westlands Ministries, an all-volunteer program, involves a feeding program for 60 to 80 children, as well as educational, health, housing, and recreational services. Boys in our ethnographic research spoke approvingly of food, schooling, and medical assistance provided by this program.

Swadener herself started an arts media project in which the children drew and painted local scenes, with violence sometimes evident in them (September 1995, p. 2). After some months Swadener and her child artists put up a display and sale of their art at Utamaduni Crafts in Langata and the Sarit Center in Westlands. Later activities involved some of the children's mothers who live in Kangemi, where they make crafts. Subsequent activities included a choir and drama performance based on street life. Some of the boys went on to become apprenticed to a professional sculptor with an eye to a professional career of their own. Swadener writes retrospectively:

After a couple of weeks of working with the kids, mostly boys ranging in age from 7 to 18, I noted that they were most "engaged" with the arts materials. I decided to expand on this and in early October began planning for our first art and crafts exhibit. The young artists made greeting cards, paintings and drawings, and my daughter and I did tie-dyeing with the boys in the group home. My husband brought in professional artists he knew to serve as mentors and role models, and by mid-December we had our first exhibit at Utamaduni Crafts. We provided some new clothes, shoes, and "artist" badges for the 24 proud artists most of whom were in the back of a truck as we arrived for the opening. During our weeklong show we did not make much money, but the self-esteem enhancement was obvious! We did make enough to present all the participants with an 'artist starter kit' and some clothing. The volunteers and kids truly came, and we had a successful exhibit and arts demonstration booth in the 'other side of the street' event. Our drama, choir, and talent show were well received and this time we made enough money to buy needed items for all the participants. (October 1995, pp. 1–2)

Swadener worked concurrently with street children and whenever possible their mothers too. Echoing our remarks above on family rehabilitation she concludes, "Getting to know the mothers and families of children on the street is very important particularly if the goal is to rehabilitate children and get them off the street and back into school" (September 1995, p. 2). While it is clear that art projects do not yield large sums of money, Swadener and her associates consistently observed pleasure and believed that she raised self-esteem among the children, a worthy enough outcome aside from economic considerations.

One of Swadener's former students was featured in a *Daily Nation* story on Saturday, February 27, 1999, by Fred Mbugua. This 20-year-old boy now is back on the streets, after Swadener's program had financial problems, although he continues with his art. Under Swadener's program, he was trained as a sculpture and housed for two years while in training. Presently he uses his money to buy his materials, some of which are currently on show. Nevertheless, "He will be sleeping in the bush again tonight. If his tomorrow comes, he will carve some more" (p. 8). Clearly art alone, while providing a meaningful pursuit, is insufficient without simultaneously addressing economic concerns for gaining a livelihood. Swadener makes a special advocacy for volunteerism. She writes, "The majority of our activities are carried out by volunteers, most of whom are Kenyan, but also have been from Germany, Canada, and the U.S.A . . . also included are children from local schools, who tutored, performed . . . others told Bible stories, teach AIDS prevention and work on non-violent conflict resolution" (September 1995, p. 2).

NATIONAL ISSUES

Our discussion so far of community-based programs clearly shows that often a national and an international component are at work too. It is for this reason that our model of levels of social organization emphasizes an interaction dynamic, especially as this is necessary for successful application and outcomes. Consideration of the national level first invites consideration of high-level national policies by the government that have contributed directly to the rise of street children problems in the first place. A national commitment to reversing these policies would help to resolve the street children problems. At the same time, Kenya remains a "dependent" nation, depending on the goodwill and overly political whims of foreign so-called "donor" nations. National global interactions are crucial, for example, in determining street children policy, not to mention other programs such as AIDS research, food, and women's issues, since these are of current concern to many foreign countries. In fact, many Europeans and Americans know only that African countries have many AIDS victims, famished children including street children, and female circumcision. While we in no way wish to minimize these social problems, the African human environment is far more complicated than simple Western stereotypes. For this reason, we have consciously described the typical street child in Kenya as first a child, one with a child's aspirations for school, and one who often is best understood, like many other Kenyans, as a member of the working poor. Programs to help all Kenyan children and poor people also help street children. Nevertheless, although global politics and power are intimately interrelated with Kenya's fate (consider tourism, too), it remains that Kenyans do have agency and ultimate control over their own public policy. Some of the causes arguably associated with the rise of street children due to national-level policies indicate at least the following: an overemphasis on urban development at the expense of rural development, abandonment of universal education as a public entitlement, and failure to control "tribal clashes" with consequent displaced refugees. On the positive side, governmental policy has advocated family planning with recent evidence that population growth has been reversed.   Nevertheless, government policies have often supported roundups of children for forced residence in camps along with toleration through benign neglect of police brutality and efforts to "criminalize" street children. Government-run approved schools and remand institutions, for example, figure prominently in the lives of street children in our research. As we have seen, police brutality is a common experience, too, a common fear expressed by both boys and girls in our study.

We propose here specific suggestions at the national level of government policy. There should be more focus on rural development and implementation of universal education, issues that will certainly benefit all Kenyans.   We propose reforms in the law and criminal justice systems, including the police. There is a need to address corruption associated with street children projects and others, too. Importantly government can undertake a policy of public education about the complexities of social life lived by street children so as to reduce stigma and exclusive perception of street children as criminals. Perhaps the national education curriculum could contain teaching units on street children. Nationally run radio and television can play an important role in public education. Street children are, in fact, Kenya citizens and deserve an accurate portrayal of their situation. Of these suggestions made here for reform, we feel that since reform of the police and justice system is of immediate concern to street children, and is our view, too, it should receive top priority.

Justice System

At the moment in Kenya the street child by and large is a "symbol" of the criminal element. Urban crime, especially violent crime, is certainly a realistic problem in the public imagination and is a perceived urban reality. Although many street children engage in petty crime, they are rarely members of armed gangs, against whom most neighborhoods in Kenya have erected high walls and fences and positioned attack dogs. White-collar crime, especially corruption in public institutions, water resources, lands, and public registries sometimes brings, for example, Kenya's water supplies and other services to a standstill. Purse snatching and glue sniffing pale in comparison to some of the more serious crimes now taking place in the country. In Kenya, urban crimes account for over 50% of nonviolent and violent cases, even though most of Kenya is rural.   While this trend of criminality could be attributed to the fact that reporting of crimes in rural areas is limited due to the absence of or the limited access to the police and courts, it is still arguable that the changes resulting from modernization and urbanization have mainly affected urban more than rural areas.

The offenses committed by juveniles range from misdemeanors to felonies, as evidenced by petty theft, vandalism or damage of property, housebreaking, use and possession of liquors, being idle and disorderly, defilement of minor girls, drug abuse (e.g., sniffing of glue or smoking of cannabis sativa), robbery with violence, manslaughter, and so forth. The delinquents are usually apprehended by the police or reported to the probation officers, the children's officers, or the chiefs so that they can be taken to the courts, after which they could be sent to the approved schools. While not wanting to deny street children's criminal activities, we do want to muddy the waters by advocating here that the street child can also be reconstructed as a "symbol" of the working poor. Many young girls work as housemaids, too, often in oppressive and exploitative circumstances. Boys and girls continue to illegally work on tea and coffee plantations where minor workers are often exploited.

Street girls, while generally not working as garbage collectors, are frequently victimized as child prostitutes with no reproach for their sexual exploiters. Instead, it is the street girls who go to jail in large numbers. The *Weekly Review* (October 28, 1994, p. 42), for example, reports that a survey among street girls found 68% had been in an official place of detention like remand homes or police cells. They commonly reported beatings, abuse, and unsanitary conditions. We have commented earlier on the jail experience of girls in our own research. David Orr, in a story in the *Christian Science Monitor* (March 19, 1997, p. 7) about Nairobi street children abused by law officers in Kenya, writes that the African Network for the Prevention and Protection Against Child Abuse and Neglect (ANPPCAN) "estimates that as many as 120 street children appear before Nairobi Juvenile Court each week. For boys, the charge is usually vagrancy; for girls, loitering with intent" (citing Elizabeth Oyugi of ANPPCAN). Orr continues, "The police seem to think that all street children are thieves . . . most of them complain of having been beaten by the police" (1997, p. 7). Concerning more general public violence discussed previously, we have presented our materials involving police violence, including the example of Simon, whose investigation was stonewalled by the authorities, a situation not unusual when street children are victimized. The alleged murderer of Simon was eventually set free.

Clearly a vigorous program of disciplinary intervention by those in authority is needed to address the problem of police brutality directed, often without cause, at street children. Law reform in areas of the law pertaining to children should be another priority in an attempt to assist street children by improving the legal status of all children. Justice Effie Owuor of the Kenyan Court of Appeal writes, "A large body of present laws on children dates back to the colonial period, and for this reason such law is defective in many respects. Since the colonial government was mainly concerned with orderly governance rather than with popular social aspirations, its legislative intervention was essentially mischief-oriented and not positively geared towards the improvement of the condition of the child (1994, p. 7). According to Justice Owour, current legislation on children focuses on the following concerns: employment laws, prohibition of oppressive contracts, provision of life's essentials, prohibition of exploitation including child harassment, and guarantee of rights in civic process and laws that provide for the protection and discipline of the child. Problems arise because these laws sometimes run counter to religious and customary standards prevalent in Kenya. Street children are most directly impacted by the Children and Young Person Act, which overlaps with the Borstal Institutions Act. These laws regulate juvenile courts, discipline of children, and remand or rehabilitation institutions. Despite over 60 parliamentary enactments, Justice Owuor believes that there is no single national policy on children. Justice Owuor heads a law reform commission study, which is investigating how best to conduct and improve domestic child law, including problems associated with the street children's place in the wider society and legal system. Improving the legal rights of children closely parallels the need to reform gender imbalances in Kenyan law. Children born out of wedlock, some of whom are street children, are the legal responsibility of their mothers only. Fathers have no legal responsibility for their illegitimate children. On this point, Janet Kabeberi (1990) states:

Children born out of wedlock are considered legitimate only after the natural parents are married to each other lawfully. The duty to maintain these children in Kenya primarily lies upon the mother alone. The repeal of the Affiliation Act in 1969 saw the end of that legal duty on the part of the natural father. The effect of the repeal of this Act was to relieve putative fathers of children born out of wedlock of the responsibility to maintain and support them until the attainment of majority age." (p. 31)

GLOBAL INTEGRATION

The previous pages have contained some examples as to how global integration has played itself out on the ground in Kenya. We want to emphasize the importance of and also to applaud integrative efforts that take into account that internationally initiated programs, by governments, the United Nations, private volunteers, and so on need to be especially sensitive to the significance of "cultural models" and not unilaterally impose Western values in the case of family planning programs, which do not take into account African ideas about ideal family size or proper family structure. Based on empirical research, Annabel Erulkar (1998) concludes that the ideal family size in Kenya is four children, 2 boys and 2 girls, not the unspecified presumably intended reduction, to 2 or fewer children, favored in the West and now built into many Western-funded family planing programs. Similarly, is it possible that reinvented polygyny, along the lines of indigenous regulated marriage practices, might be better for children than the current chaotic form of unregulated polygyny common in Kenya today (Kilbride, 1994; Suda, 1997)? Would Western funding sources support the polygynous family as a way to bolster the traditional African family if this were to be seen in the interest of women and children? More specifically, is this even a question that can be raised for research given the ideological commitment that Western women hold for monogamy (see Sudarkasa, 1982)? Certainly in the past, Kenya polygyny was one of the reasons all children without exception had a father involved in his or her life.

Cultural models aside, it is clear that power, money, and influence now clearly reside primarily in the West regarding control over the machinery and direction of most rehabilitative and prevention programs. For this reason, all must be on guard against some Kenyans who, for personal gain, sometimes silently acquiesce to policies at odds with cultural values that they privately hold and others who, given power imbalances, are fearful of resisting the implementation of such policies by international agencies. Participation without cultural critique does not fully take advantage of potential Kenyan contributions to internationally initiated development projects concerning street children and other topics.

Corruption

Today in Kenya there is an especially problematic dimension associated with corruption that affects horizontal linkage. There is a growing attitude in Kenya that the entire society has been reduced to a kind of "global beggar status." We noted above that Bishop Kuria, for instance, wishes to reverse unnecessary dependence on outside assistance, which, as we suggest here, not only creates dependency but also compliance with outside cultural agendas too. For example, in a recent position paper, Benson Wambugu reported that the German ambassador to Kenya characterized Kenya as a global beggar primarily because of corruption (*The People*, February 13, 1999, pp. 1 and 2). Addressing a variety of examples, including tourism, petrol importation, cashew nut parastatal plants, coffee production, local butter production, the Mombasa port, and Kenyatta International Airport, among others, Ambassador Michael Gerdts made his case that "the criminal energy that goes into corruption and mega corruption is one of the most creative forces in the country, too often . . . the government does not receive what it is entitled to and often what it receives is often redirected into private pockets" (p. 2). The Ambassador warned Kenyans against continuing to be too dependant on donor funding and, echoing Bishop Kuria's voice, advised that Kenya use its own resources, which he considers to be considerable, in a more efficient fashion than presently.

Given the extent to which Kenyans are, in fact, captivated by a "donor mentality," one model of street children regarding their specific social status in the wider Kenyan society would conceptualize them as at the bottom of a status hierarchy of beggars, their begging is merely more blatant and direct in comparison to the more sophisticated styles used by more wealthy and cosmopolitan Kenyans to manipulate donor resources into their pockets. We hasten to add, however, that the vast majority of Kenyans are not beggars and regrettably are hindered from gaining from the numerous development programs targeted for them by the corrupt practices of some of their fellow countrymen, who sometimes go begging for international support for their private gains.

Corruption sometimes rears its ugly head in programs involving street children. An administrator, as previously noted, familiar with one of the feeding centers in Korogocho indicated that a donation from Germany in the form of a Land Rover wound up being used several hundred miles from Nairobi transporting crops to market by a member of the family of one of the board members of the feeding center. In another example among many known to the writers, an American institution, for example, reports receiving an exaggerated personal appeal for street children assistance through the mail that was obviously fabricated. This appeal, received from an NGO based in the slums of Nairobi, states, "We usually feed them both spiritually and with normal food, and teach them hygiene by washing their clothes, trimming their nails and hair, and teaching them basic agriculture (planting, weeding, knowing food crops, irrigating, etc.). Among other developmental activities we are proceeding with, we have tailoring, kiosk, hair salons, AIDS-volunteers, etc."

In addition to a staggering array of programs, this appeal claimed, "All street children (in Kenya) will be collected and will be professionally trained starting with areas at Nairobi City." Street children are seen in this letter as victims of "humanistic devilish behavior" resulting from their sharing garbage with "mosquitoes, houseflies, cockroaches, dog, cats, etc." The appeal is "officially stamped" by seal, a Kenyan practice, with a personal signature of the "Executive Chairman" to whom the request of 36,779,587 shillings should be sent (about US $600,000!). Needless to say, the budget categories were extremely superficial (including 75,000 shillings for a computer, 3,000,000 shillings for "education," 2,000,000 shillings for "health," and 1,500,000 shillings for "miscellaneous services"). Indeed, international appeals to assist street children are now big business. Not all efforts, of course, involve corruption; most are legitimate appeals to help street children. On a global scale, we learn from Tobias Hecht concerning Brazil, for example, that "lucrative direct mail campaigns have been launched in the United States to raise money for projects with street children . . . Covenant House raised more than U.S. $28 million in this way" (1998, p. 3).

Corruption is, as we have noted before, a special and serious problem in Kenya against which there was created in 1998, if only for symbolic purposes, an "anticorruption" authority. International programs for street children, depending as they do on people's genuine concern for the well-being of children, also open up the possibility for corrupt individuals to prey upon such sentiments. Therefore, "top-down" linkages from global programs must be prepared to guard against corruption at the national and local levels from those who are deceptive and in a position to take advantage of such well-intentioned concern.

Elimination of corruption, however, is more complex than simply making a moral commitment to do so although this would help. Corruption in Africa, for example, differs from that of Asia.   In Africa, state institutions are comparatively weak, as well as autocratic, thus giving rise to uncoordinated and therefore diffuse and competitive corruption (Collier and Gunning, 1999). Corruption in African countries such as Kenya contrasts with the centralized and less diffuse and more predictable corruption found in Asian countries. Contributing to corruption in Africa is a comparatively high level of ethnic fragmentation. Strikingly, on a measure of fractionalization, it was found that "the average African country is more than twice as fractionalized as other developing regions" (Collier and Gunning, 1999, p. 67). National economic development is also heavily dependent on infrastructure such as repairs to transportation services and associated technologies.   Nevertheless, while realizing that corruption is embedded in social and political institutions, it is imperative to address corruption as a prime priority in contributing to an improvement in the delivery of services and programs specifically for street children. All children will be uplifted along with all Kenyans to the extent that a holistic policy is pursued whereby corruption is reduced, infrastructure developed, fragmentation lessened, and state autocracy resisted.

While being on guard against corruption, it must also be emphasized that the present marginal position of Kenya in the global economy, a historical situation significantly linked to the origin of street children in Kenya, has much to do with the legacy of colonialism. Little wonder that the letter of appeal described previously, obviously exaggerated for personal gain notwithstanding, was based on an unrealistic estimate of the wealth of individuals and institutions in the West.   Such an image was reinforced by a colonial history of privilege and separation where Europeans and Americans in Kenya are virtually always excessively wealthy compared to Africans. It cannot be emphasized enough to underscore the fact that there are no European or Asian street children in Kenya, or at least we have never seen one.

Debt Relief

In an earlier chapter, along with exploitative work policies for child workers, we described how colonial labor policy served to break up families. Such child labor abuses, of which the street children problem is but a special case, continue today. We have argued here that international policies to help street children must consider how helping all children and the working poor in Kenya will also have a positive impact on the street child. This is largely a preventive argument. As Bishop Kuria has pointed out and we ourselves have seen, international programs alone are not enough. The bishop also advocates Kenyan national agency.   At the same time, nevertheless, might one also appeal to the consciousness of the West to atone for its past self-motivated policies and economic gains in colonialism (Rodney, 1974). Such an attitude would, for example, provide a basis for forgiving some past Kenyan debts to Western nations, so as to improve Kenya's economic potential and, thereby, help street children and the rest of the poor.

It should also be noted that current economic problems in Africa, including Kenya, have been exacerbated by strict austerity measures imposed in the last fifteen years by "structural adjustment" programs instituted by the World Bank and the International Monetary Fund. While there are some advantages in improved austerity measures, such as a lessening of overreliance on inefficient government agencies, the overall effect has been negative for Africa's poor and most vulnerable people. For example, observers of structural adjustment programs in Kenya have documented a negative impact on children (Swadener, Kabiru, & Njenga, n.d.; Gakuru, 1995). Malnutrition and an increased child mortality rate are on the increase in Kenya since structural adjustments were imposed. Aptly, the phrase "children in debt" is used by UNICEF to characterize the risk structural adjustment measures have imposed on children in many nations of the world (Swadener, Kabiru, & Njenga; n.d.).

A consistent appeal by street children for educational opportunities, which we have documented, is unlikely to be addressed given that Kenya, as well as other African nations, is experiencing an educational crisis for most children. A recent report by the human rights group OXFAM entitled *Education Now: Break the Cycle of Poverty* (1999) identifies Africa as having 24 of the world's worst-performing nations in providing educational opportunities for children. The report said serious thought should be given to the relief of international debts, which are much greater than national education budgets in African countries. In fact, there is an increasing awareness in the West that debt reduction (or total forgiveness) is in the best interest of all concerned. In an article in the *Philadelphia Inquirer*, Sonya Ross reports that while addressing a meeting of African government officials, President Bill Clinton said that he would propose that the world's industrialized nations develop a plan to forgive $70 billion in debt. The President said, "Our goal is to ensure that no country committed to fundamental reforms is left with a debt burden that keeps it from meeting its people's basic human needs" (March 17, 1998, p. 12). To finance debt relief, President Clinton proposes to sell some gold reserves held by the International Monetary Fund and World Bank. We strongly endorse such a global perspective concerning the plight of street children described in this book. Surely such "children in debt" are clearly within the practical reach of all citizens of wealthier, industrialized nations who want to help our youngest citizens and their families to help themselves so that in the future they will need no help from others. Ideally those who now are street children will someday be in a position to help others in need. Our study of street children in Kenya has described what life is like for those children from an "outsider's" point of view as well as from the point of view of the street children themselves. Problems and possible solutions have been offered. Our challenge now is to turn this cycle of poverty into a cycle of prosperity with concern for the well-being of all.

Bibliography

Adams, A. R. (1994). Sibling interactions between street children in Nairobi, Kenya. Unpublishsed research report. Bryn Mawr College summer research report.

Adepoju, A. (1997). *Family population and development in Africa*. London: Zed Books.

Agar, M. (1996). *The professional strangers: An informal introduction to ethnography.* New York: Academic Press.

AIDS CAP/Family Health International. (1996). *AIDS in Kenya: Socioeconomic impact and policy Implications USAID.*

Anthony, E. (1987). Risk, vulnerability and resilience: An overview. In E. Anthony & B. Cohler (Eds.), *The invulnerable child* (pp. 3–49). New York: Guilford Press.

Anthony, E., & Cohler, B. (Eds.). (1987). *The invulnerable child.* New York: Guilford Press.

Aptekar, L. (1988). *The street children of Cali.* Durham, NC: Duke University Press.

Aswani, H. (1972). Luhya (Bunyore) oral literature. In Taban Lo Liyong (Eds.), *Popular culture in East Africa.* Nairobi, Kenya: Longman.

Bambrah, G. K. (1996). Mombasa municipal consultation on urban poverty reduction. Paper prepared for the Municipal Council of Mombasa, April 10–12.

Bamurange, V. (1998). Relationships for survival—young mothers and street youths. In Magodalena Rwebangira & Rita Liljestrom (Eds.), *Haraka Look before you leap: Youth at the crossroad of custom and modernity* (pp. 221–247). Stockholm: Nordiska Afrikainstitutet.

Behar, R., & Gordon, D. A. (Eds.). (1995). *Women writing culture.* Berkeley: University of California Press.

Bernard, H. R. (1994). *Research methods in anthropology: Qualitative and quantitative approaches.* Thousand Oaks, CA: Sage Publications.

Bourdillon, M .F. C. (1991). *Harassed but very much alive.* Zimbabwe: Mambo Press.

Bourgois, P. (1996). Confronting anthropology, education, and inner city apartheid. *American Anthropologist, 98, 2,* 249–265.

Bradley, C. (1997). Why fertility is going down in Maragoli. In T. Weisner, C. Bradley, & P. Kilbride (Eds.), *African families and the crisis of social change* (pp. 227–252). Westport, CT: Bergin and Garvey.

Bradshaw, Y. W., Kaiser, P. J. & Ndegwa, S. N. (1995, September). Rethinking theoretical and methodological approaches to the study of African development. *African Studies Review, 38,* 2, 39-65.

Bwibo, M. (1982). Battered child syndrome. In P. Onyango & D. Kayongo-Male (Eds.), *Child labour and health* (pp. 2-13). Nairobi: Acme Press.

Campos, R., Antunes, C., Raffaelli, M., Halsey, N., Greco, W., Greco, M., Greco, D., Rolf, J., & Ruff, A. (1994). Social networks and daily activities of street youth in Belo Horizonte, Brazil. *Child Development, 65,* 319-330.

Cattell, M. (1997). The discourse of neglect: Family support for the elderly in Samia. In T. Weisner, C. Bradley, and P. Kilbride (Eds.) *African families and the crisis of social change* (pp. 157–184). Westport, CT: Bergin and Garvey.

Central Bureau of Statistics. (1998*). Poverty in Kenya: Poverty and social indicators.* Nairobi: Government Press.

Clifford, J., & Marcus, G. E. (Eds.) (1986). *Writing culture: The politics and poetics of ethnography.* Berkeley: University of California Press.

Collier, P., & Gunning, J. W. (1999, March). Explaining African economic performance. *Journal of Economic Literature, 37,* pp. 64–111.

Da Matta, R. (1994). Some biased remarks on interpretivism: A view from Brazil. In R. Borofsky (Ed.), *Assessing cultural anthropology* (pp. 119–133). New York: McGraw-Hill.

Dehavenon, A. (Ed.). (1996). *There's no place like home: Anthropological perspectives on housing and homelessness in the United States.* Westport, CT: Bergin and Garvey.

Desjarlais, R. (1996, June). Some causes and cultures of homelessness. *American Anthropologist, 98,* 2, 420-425.

Dodge, C. P., & Raundalen, M. (1991). *Reaching children in war Sudan, Uganda and Mozambique.* Norway: Sigma Forlag.

Egan, S. (Ed.) (1987). S.M. Otieno: Kenya's unique burial saga. Nairobi: A Nation Newspapers Publication.

Erulkar, A. S. (1998). *Adolescent experiences and lifestyles in Central Province Kenya.* Nairobi: Population Council.

Gakuru, O. N. (1995). Early childhood care and development: Formative research and quality in the programme for children in Kenya. Paper presented at the Conference on Environment of the Child, Bernard van Leer Foundation.

Geertz, C. (1983). *Local knowledge.* New York: Basic Books.

Geertz, C. (1988). *Works and lives: The anthropologist as authors.* Stanford, CA: Stanford University Press.

Glasser, I. (1994). *Homelessness in global perspective.* New York: G. K. Hall.

Goffman, E. (1982). *Interaction ritual: Essays on face to face behavior.* New York: Pantheon Books.

Grant, S. (1991). "Fostering—Do you have what it takes!" *Sasa: The voice of children, 1,* 2–5.

Grier, B. (1996, November). Street kids in Zimbabwe: The historical origins of a contemporary problem. Paper presented at the Annual Meeting of the African Studies Association; San Francisco, California.

Groce, C. (1993). "Nairobi street children and sheng." Unpublished research report. Bryn Mawr College, Department of Anthropology, Bryn Mawr, PA.

Gruduah, O. (1995, June 30). They survive by selling garbage. East African Standard, p. 22.

Hakansson, T. (1988). *Bridewealth, women and land: Social change among the Gusii of Kenya.* Uppsala Series in Cultural Anthropology, 10. Uppsala, Kenya: Uppsala University.

Harris, M. (1994). Cultural materialism is alive and well and won't go away until something better comes along.   In R. Borofsky (Ed.), *Assessing cultural anthropology.* New York: McGraw-Hill.

Hearing on street children in Kenya. (1995). *Report on a hearing held in Nairobi, Kenya, November 4-5, 1994.* Nairobi: African Network for the Prevention and Protection Against Child Abuse and Neglect.

Hecht, T. (1998). *At home in the street: Street children of northeast Brazil.* New York: Cambridge University Press.

Helping hand for the destitute. (1998, January 14). *Daily Nation,* p. 3.

Holmquist, F., Weaver, F., & Ford, M. (1994). The structural development of Kenya's political economy. *African Studies Review, 31,* 69–107.

Hopper, K., & Baumohl, J. (1994). Redefining the cursed: A historical interpretation of American Homelessness. In J. Baumohl (Ed.), *Homelessness in America.* Phoenix, AZ: Arizona Oryx Press.

Horchler, M. (1993). A look at the role of the church with respect to the street children problem in Kenya. Unpublished research report. Bryn Mawr College, Department of Anthropology, Bryn Mawr College, Bryn Mawr, PA.

Jackson, J. E. (1990). I am a Fieldnote: Fieldnotes as a symbol of professional identity. In R. Sanjek (Ed.), *Fieldnotes* (pp. 3–34). Ithaca, NY: Cornell University Press.

Kabeberi, J. (1990). *The child: Custody, care and maintenance.* Nairobi: Oxford University Press.

Kamau, M. (1996, August).   Kuria's hope for street children.   *The People,* Feature Section.

Kayongo-Male, D., & Walji, P. (1984). *Children at work in Kenya.* Nairobi: Oxford University Press.

Kenyatta, J. (1965). *Facing Mt. Kenya: The tribal life of the Gikuyu.* New York: Vintage Books.

Kilbride, P. (1986). *Cultural persistence and socio-economic change among the Abaluyia: Some modern problems in patterns of child care.* Nairobi: Gideon S. Were Press.

Kilbride, P. (1991). Female violence against related children: Infanticide as a modern form of deviance in Kenya. In M. Freilich, D. Raybeck, & J. Savishinsky (Eds.), *Deviance: Anthropological perspectives* (pp. 115–133). Westport, CT: Bergin and Garvey.

Kilbride, P. (1992). Unwanted children as a consequence of delocalization in modern Kenya. In J. Poggie, W. Dewalt, & W. Dressler (Eds.), *Anthropological research: Process and application* (pp. 185-203).   Albany: State University of New York Press.

Kilbride, P. (1994). *Plural marriage for our times: A re-invented option.* Westport, CT: Bergin and Garvey.

Kilbride, P., & Kilbride, J. (1990). *Changing family life in East Africa: Women and children at risk.* University Park, PA: Pennsylvania State University Press.

Kilbride, J., & Kilbride, P. (1994). To have and to share: Culturally constituted fostering in familial settings. In J. Blacher (Ed.), *When there's no place like home: Options for children living apart from their families* (pp. 321–329). Baltimore, MD: Paul H. Brookes Publishing.

Kilbride, P., & Kilbride, J. (1997). Stigma, role overload, and delocalization among contemporary Kenyan women. In T. Weisner, C. Bradley, & P. Kilbride (Eds.), *African families in the crisis of social change* (pp. 208–227). Westport, CT: Bergin and Garvey.

Le Roux, J. (1996). Street children in South Africa: Findings from interviews on the background of street children in Pretoria, South Africa. *Adolescence, 31*, 122, 423–431.

LiJembe, J. (1967). The valley between: A Muluyia's story. In L. K. Fox (Ed.), *East African Childhood: Three versions* (pp. 1–45). London: Oxford University Press.

Like mother, like daughter. (1994, October 28). *The Weekly Review*, p. 42.

Lillis, K. (1992). Urbanization and education in Nairobi, Kenya. *African Urban Quarterly, 7*, 1 & 2, 68–79.

Limcuando, V. (1994). Ethnographic observations of street children in Nairobi. Unpublished research report. Bryn Mawr College, Department of Anthropology, Bryn Mawr, PA.

Lloyd, B., & Blanc, A. (1995). Children's schooling in sub-Saharan Africa. Working papers No. 78. Nairobi: The Population Council.

lo Liyong, T. (1972). *Popular culture of East Africa*. Nairobi: Longman.

Lwanga, G. (n.d.). *Health worker report*. Nangina Hospital, Kenya.

Marcus, G. E. (1994). After the critique of ethnography: Faith, hope, and charity, but the greatest of these is charity. In R. Borofsky (Ed.), *Assessing cultural anthropology*. New York: McGraw-Hill.

Mbugua, F. (1999, February 27). A tale of two city lives. *Daily Nation*, p. 8.

Merton, R., Fiske, M., & Kendall, P. (1990). *The focused interview: A manual of problems and procedures*. New York: Free Press.

Miller, C. (1971). *The lunatic express*. New York: Ballantine Books.

Ministry of Education. (1999). *Statistical data on enrollment and drop out rates*. Statistics section. Nairobi: Government of Kenya.

Ministry of Health. (1994). *AIDS in Kenya: Backgrounds, projections, impact and interventions*. Prepared by the National AIDS Control Programme, Ministry of Health and National Council for Population and Development. Nairobi: Government of Kenya.

Muchungu, C. (1998, January 11). Micro loan scheme uplifts slum women. *Daily Nation*.

Mukoyogo, C., & Williams, G. (1993). *AIDS orphans: A community perspective from Tanzania*. Actionaid, AMREF, and World in Need. Oxford: Parchment Ltd. Strategies for Hope, 5.

Mulder, M. (1992). Women's Strategies in Polygynous Marriage. *Human Nature 3*(1): 45–70.

Munroe, R., & Munroe, R. (1971). Household density and infant care in an East African society. *Journal of Social Psychology, 83*, 3–13.

Mwangi, M. (1976). *Going down river road*. Nairobi: East African Educational Publishers Ltd.

Nasimiyu, R. (1997). Changing women's rights over property in western Kenya. In T. Weisner, C. Bradley, & P. Kilbride (Eds.), *African families and the crisis of social change* (pp. 283-299). Westport, CT: Bergin and Garvey.

Ndirangu, W. (1994). *Rehabilitation of young street girls*. Nairobi: Rescue Dada Center.

Ngesa, M. (1999, February 24). Huruma residents living in garbage. *East African Standard*, p. 24.

Njeru, E., Kariuki, P., & Kilbride, P. (1995, August). Because we are street children: Voices from the streets of Nairobi. Paper presented for the third interfaculty collaboration program. The University of Nairobi Conference on Social Behavior and Health.

Obudho, R. A. (1992). The role of metropolitan Nairobi in spatial planning of Kenya: Towards a planning alternative. *African Urban Quarterly, 7,* 1 & 2, 210–217.

Obudho, R. A., & Aduwo, G. O. (1992). The nature of the urbanization process and urbanism in the city of Nairobi, Kenya. *African Urban Quarterly, 7,* 1 & 2, 50–64.

Odegi-Awuondo, C., Namai, H., & Mutsotso, B. (1994). *Masters of survival.* Nairobi: Basic Books.

Okwembah, A. (1998, June 5). Centre brings hope for street children. *Daily Nation,* p. 23.

Ominde, S. (1952). *The Luo girl: From infancy to marriage.* Nairobi: East Africa Literature Bureau.

Orr, D. (1997, March 19). Nairobi street children abused by law officers. *Christian Science Monitor.*

Otieno, F.A.O. (1992). Solid waste management in the city of Nairobi; What are the prospects for the future? *African Urban Quarterly, 7,* 1 & 2, 142–151.

Owuor, E. (1994). Children in the context of law: An African experience. Unqualified manuscript. High Court of Kenya, Nairobi, Kenya.

Oxfam. (1999). Education Now: Break the cycle of poverty.

Parkin, D., & Nyamwaya, D. (1987). *Transformation of African marriage.* Manchester, UK: Manchester University Press.

Pelto, P. J., & Pelto, G. H. (1978). *Anthropological research: The structure of inquiry.* Cambridge: Cambridge University Press.

Raybeck, D. (1991. Hard versus soft deviance: Anthropology and labeling theory. In M. Freilich, D. Raybeck, & J. Savishinsky (Eds.), *Deviance: Anthropological perspectives* (pp. 51–73). Westport, CT: Bergin and Garvey.

Rodney, W. (1974). *How Europe underdeveloped Africa.* Washington, DC: Harvard University Press.

Ross, S. (1998, March 17). Commentary. *Philadelphia Inquirer,* p. 12.

Salzman, P. (1998). *The anthropology of real life: Events in human experience.* Prospect Heights, IL: Waveland Press.

Sanjek, R. (Ed.). (1990). *Fieldnotes: The makings of anthropology.* Ithaca, NY: Cornell University Press.

Saoke, P., & Mutemi, R. (1994). *Needs assessment of children orphaned by* AIDS: A study Funded by UNICEF Kenya Country Office.

Scheper-Hughes, N., & Hoffman, D. (1998). Brazilian apartheid: Street kids and the struggle for urban space. In N. Scheper-Hughes & C. Sargent (Eds.), *Small wars: The cultural politics of childhood* (pp. 352–389). Berkeley: University of California Press.

Scheper-Hughes, N., & Sargent, C. (Eds.). (1998*). Small wars: The cultural politics of childhood.* California: University of California Press.

Scheper-Hughes, N., & Sargent, C. (Eds.). (1998). Introduction. In *Small wars: The cultural politics of childhood* (pp. 1–35). Berkeley: University of California Press.

Shorter, A. (1991). *The church in the African city.* New York: Orbis Books.

Situma, F. (1992). The environmental problems in the city of Nairobi, Kenya. *African Urban Quarterly, 7,* 1 & 2, 167–177.

Snow, D., & Anderson, L. (1993). *Down on their luck: A study of homeless street people* (pp. 268–283). Westport, CT: Bergin and Garvey.

Suda, C. (1994, January).   Report of a baseline survey on street children in Nairobi,Kenya. Child welfare society of Kenya, Nairobi.

Suda, C. (1997). Street children in Nairobi and the African cultural ideology of kin-based support system: Change and challenge. *Child Abuse Review, 6,* 199–217.

Suda, C. (1999, April). African family and child welfare: Tradition in transition. *International Journal of Contemporary Sociology, 36,* 1, 56-65.

Sudarkasa, N. (1982).   African and Afro-American family structure. In J. B. Cole (Ed.), *Anthropology for the eighties.* New York: The Free Press.

Susser, I. (1996). The construction of poverty and homelessness in U.S. cities. *Annual Reviews of Anthropology, 25,* 411–435.

Swadener, B., Kabiru, M., & Njenga, A. (n.d.). Does the village still raise the children? A collaborative study of changing childrearing and early education in Kenya. Book manuscript in preparation.

Swadener, B. (1995, September). Observations from the street—strategies that work with street children. *African Regional ECCE Journal.*

Swadener, B. (1995, October). Observations from the street— strategies that work with street children. *Anthropology Newsletter.* American Anthropological Association.

Swadener, B., Kabiru, M., & Njenga, A. (1996). Changing child-rearing practices and community mobilization for young children and families. In *Kenya: A collaborative study.* Nairobi: National Center for Early Childhood Education.

Swart, J. (1990). *Malunde: The street children of Hillbron.* Johannesburg, South Africa: Witwatersrand University Press.

Syagga, P., & Kiamba, J. (1992).   Housing the urban poor: A case study of Pumwani, Kibera and Dandora Estates in the City of Nairobi, Kenya. *African Urban Quarterly,* 7, 1 & 2, 79–90.

Undugu Society of Kenya.   Nairobi, Kenya. (n.d.). *Despair and hope in the slums of Nairobi.*

Wagner, D. (1993). *Checkerboard square: Culture and resistance in a homeless community.* Boulder: Westview Press.

Wagner, G. (1949). *The Bantu of North Kavirondo.* Vol. 1. London: Oxford University Press for International African Institute.

Wagner, G. (1956). *The Bantu of North Kavirondo.* Vol. 2. London: Oxford University Press for International African Institute.

Wambugu, B. (1999, February 13). Commentary. *The People,* pp. 1 & 2.

Weisner, T. (1982). Sibling interdependence and child caretaking: A cross-cultural view. In M. Lamb & B. Sutton-Smith (Eds.), *Sibling relationships: Their nature and significance across the lifespan* (pp. 305–327). Hillsdale, NJ: Lawrence Erlbaum

Weisner, T. (1987). Socialization for parenthood in sibling caretaking societies. In J. Lancaster, J. Altmann, A. Rossi, & L. Sherrod (Eds.), *Parenting across the lifespan: Biosocial dimensions* (pp. 237-270). New York: Aldine De Gruyter.

Weisner, T., Bradley, C., & Kilbride, P. (Eds.) (1997). *African families in crisis of social change.* Westport, CT: Bergin and Garvey.

Weston, K. (1991). *Families we choose.* New York: Columbia University Press.

Wolf, M. (1992). *A thrice told tale: Feminism, post modernism and ethnographic responsibility.* Stanford, CA: Stanford University Press.

Wolford, P., (1996, September 27). No place to spend a childhood. *Plain Dealer,* p. 12b.

Worth, S., and Adair, J. (1970). Navaho filmakers. *American Anthropologist, 72,* 1, 9-35.

Index

About the Authors

PHILIP KILBRIDE is Chair and Professor of Anthropology at Bryn Mawr College, Pennsylvania.

COLLETTE SUDA is Associate Professor of Sociology and Director, Institute of African Studies, University of Nairobi.

ENOS NJERU is Senior Lecturer in the Department of Sociology, University of Nairobi, Kenya.